ASHE Higher Education Report: ⅼ
Kelly Ward, Lisa E. Wolf-Wendel, Series Editors

M000310789

College Choice and Access to College: Moving Policies, Research, and Practice to the 21st Century

Amy Aldous Bergerson

College Choice and Access to College: Moving Policy, Research, and Practice to the 21st Century
Amy Aldous Bergerson
ASHE Higher Education Report: Volume 35, Number 4
Kelly Ward, Lisa E. Wolf-Wendel, Series Editors

ISSN 1551-6970   electronic ISSN 1554-6306   ISBN 978-0-4706-1391-7

The ASHE Higher Education Report is part of the Jossey-Bass Higher and Adult Education Series and is published six times a year by Wiley Subscription Services, Inc., A Wiley Company, at Jossey-Bass, 989 Market Street, San Francisco, California 94103-1741.

For subscription information, see the Back Issue/Subscription Order Form in the back of this volume.

CALL FOR PROPOSALS: Prospective authors are strongly encouraged to contact Kelly Ward (kaward@wsu.edu) or Lisa Wolf-Wendel (lwolf@ku.edu). See "About the ASHE Higher Education Report Series" in the back of this volume.

Visit the Jossey-Bass Web site at **www.josseybass.com.**

Printed in the United States of America on acid-free recycled paper.

The ASHE Higher Education Report is indexed in CIJE: Current Index to Journals in Education (ERIC), Current Abstracts (EBSCO), Education Index/Abstracts (H.W. Wilson), ERIC Database (Education Resources Information Center), Higher Education Abstracts (Claremont Graduate University), IBR & IBZ: International Bibliographies of Periodical Literature (K.G. Saur), and Resources in Education (ERIC).

Advisory Board

The ASHE Higher Education Report Series is sponsored by the Association for the Study of Higher Education (ASHE), which provides an editorial advisory board of ASHE members.

Contents

Executive Summary

The college-going population in the United States is growing increasingly diverse, yet higher education institutions remain stratified by race, ethnicity, and social class. In the last twenty years, research around the issue of college choice has shifted gears, from a focus on the development of comprehensive college choice models to an emphasis on issues of access and equity. Whether through influencing federal, state, and institutional policies, exploring in detail the nuances of the college choice experience for students of color and lower socioeconomic status, or developing new models that take into account students' social and cultural contexts, current research represents a trend toward eradicating the class, racial, and ethnic barriers that prevent many students from participating in the postsecondary educational environment.

This monograph examines and synthesizes literature on college choice from the last twenty years, building on Paulsen's ASHE-ERIC Higher Education Report (1990). This discussion is framed by issues of access and equity in higher education, and the recommendations provided are based on the assumption that it is the role of educators—in both K–12 and higher education—to address these issues, with the goal of increasing access to the wide range of postsecondary opportunities available in the United States for all students who choose to attend. This focus necessitates an understanding of the difference between access to college and college choice. College choice models developed in the 1970s and 1980s implied that the choice of whether and where to attend college was the same for all students as they walked through linear processes on the road to higher education. What has become clear in the last twenty years is that access to college is constrained for many students, thus making the choice process either infinitely more complicated or simply irrelevant. The choice process is not experienced equitably by all students whose educational aspirations include enrollment in higher education. This monograph outlines what the differences in these experiences look like and recommends ways to increase access to higher education for a wide range of students. To do so, it outlines the trends in current research on college choice, attends to the nuances of the college choice experience for students of color and from lower socioeconomic status, reviews current college preparation and access programs according to a framework of essential elements, and recommends areas for practice, policy, and research.

What Are Current Trends in College Choice Research?

College choice research in the last twenty years is strongly influenced by issues of access and equity. Specifically, researchers have increased their attention to how students are prepared for college, noting the differences in college preparation by race, ethnicity, and social class. This attention to social and cultural context has influenced the trend away from comprehensive models of college choice and toward the development of explanations of the college choice process that focus on the specific contexts in which students make postsecondary decisions. Finally, researchers have begun to emphasize the impact of their work on policy, whether federal, state, or institutional. Increased attention to the importance of policy reveals an assumption that the equity and access issues facing higher education require multilevel responses as well as individual attention.

How Is the College Choice Experience Different for Students of Color and Lower Socioeconomic Status?

Many factors play into the college choice process for students of color and lower socioeconomic status. One salient finding from the research is that although many of these students start with high educational aspirations, a gap exists between what they hope for and their participation in higher education. School context plays a role in this gap when tracking and lack of college preparation courses constrain the postsecondary options for students attending heterogeneous and low-income schools. Parent education and income also constrain these students' choices as limited information and lack of financial resources cloud the dream to attend college. Lack of involvement on the part of high school counselors and teachers who have the potential to motivate students and to increase their access to the necessary information also discourages these students from attending. And the current emphasis on student loans disproportionately reduces the chances of participation by students of color and lower socioeconomic status in higher education. Ultimately, the picture of the college choice process for these students is largely one of unrealized dreams and aspirations despite the stories of handfuls of students who have successfully navigated the complex college application process.

What Impact Do Current College Preparation Programs Have on Access and Equity in the College Choice Process?

An array of college preparation and access programs dot the college choice landscape, ranging from institutional and neighborhood programs largely funded by higher education institutions or private foundations to federal- and state-funded programs. Overall, the most effective programs include elements that improve students' access to information regarding college generally and financial aid specifically, include academic preparation for college-level courses that promote high educational aspirations and a sense of self-efficacy in attaining those goals, and develop the social skills necessary to navigate the higher education environment. It is also generally agreed that effective college preparation programs embrace a cultural wealth paradigm that views students and their families as holders of cultural knowledge and capital that is valued and legitimized throughout these programs. In other words, the focus is on the assets students bring to their educational experiences rather than on fixing their perceived deficits. Programs that incorporate these elements and see students as the holders of knowledge have the potential to assist students in pursuing their academic dreams. The college preparation and access programs available, however, do not begin to reach the large number of students for whom a college education appears unattainable.

What Is the Role of Practitioners in Increasing Access to College?

Recommendations for practice focus on how individuals and institutions can work to improve the college-going chances for all students interested in participating in higher education. For example, professionals who work with high school students are encouraged to operate through the cultural wealth paradigm. High school students encouraged by teachers and counselors who understand and validate their cultural backgrounds are more inclined to believe that higher education is attainable. In higher education, those working to recruit high school students to campus must also approach students with a cultural wealth perspective, noting the strengths that these students bring and understanding how their cultural background shapes their educational experiences. Specifically, college personnel who can communicate with students in several languages validate their cultural-linguistic backgrounds, and recruitment programs that include extended family reflect an understanding of the importance of familial ties to these students. Further, lack of information is a constraint on the college enrollment of students of color and lower socioeconomic status, and higher education campuses that recognize the importance of personal connections with students in the information-gathering process are better able to meet these students' needs. Although many view the increasing reliance on technology for information as a way to increase access, it is clear that the ability to ask questions and refine an understanding of the information provided is important for students of color and lower socioeconomic status. The use of technology as a primary information source is disproportionately advantageous for upper- and middle-class students. Finally, many recommendations for practice focus on the development of K–16 policies and practices to ensure a smoother transition from high school to college for a wide range of students. Practitioners from higher education institutions and K–12 schools are encouraged to work more closely as they plan for the academic preparation of students for college, the provision of postsecondary information for students, and the process of introducing students to the higher education environment. In sum, the recommendations for practice focus on using the cultural wealth perspective to recognize and validate the cultural backgrounds of a wide range of students and to develop an understanding of and the means to address the specific needs of students as they engage in the process of deciding whether and where to go to college.

Where Is the Field of College Choice Headed?

The field of college choice is poised to shape the future of postsecondary education through its impact on policy and practice that increase access to higher education for a wider range of students. A continued focus on examining the specific experiences of students of color and lower socioeconomic status as they engage in the college choice process is necessary to forming policies and practices that remove barriers to their participation in higher education. Well-designed qualitative studies have the potential to affect the field with their ability to illuminate the nuances of this experience across groups of students. A continued focus on state and federal financial aid policies is necessary to develop a better understanding of how financial resources play into the college choice process. And the further development and expansion of effective college preparation and access programs that can reach a broader spectrum of students is important. Although strides have been made in increasing diversity in higher education, the need to attend to the stratification of postsecondary education clearly continues. Future research in the area of college choice has the potential to significantly affect both policy and practice in ways that continue to address these important issues.

Foreword

In 1987, Hossler and Gallagher laid out three stages of college choice: aspirations, search, and choice. Institutions have increasingly focused on the last stage of the model—how to get students to chose their college. This focus on the last stage is driven in large part by economic realities and increasing competition in the marketplace. Institutions need tuition dollars to cover decreasing state support, declining values of endowment portfolios, and increasing costs associated with providing a high-quality education. Given this institutional interest, attention has focused on what institutions need to do to increase application numbers, improve yield, and raise institutional selectivity profiles. Focusing on these aspects of the college choice process assists institutions in augmenting their funding base directly by capturing more tuition dollars and indirectly by improving institutional prestige, stature, ranking, and market share. Given today's economic realities, it is not surprising that institutions spend time, money, and attention on the last stage of the choice process as a means to maximize the likelihood of students' choosing their school. Nor is it surprising that much of the literature on college choice seems to focus on advice regarding institutional branding, marketing, brochures, and image management—the things an institution needs to lure potential students and their parents.

Although all institutions of higher education need students and therefore need to worry about attracting them to their institution, the present focus on the needs of the institution (and the last stage of the choice process) may lead institutions to lose sight of students in the first two steps of the process. Amy

Bergerson's monograph is to be commended because it focuses its attention on the first two steps of Hossler and Gallagher's model: aspirations and search. This monograph, building on the 1990 monograph by Michael Paulsen, looks at the issue of college access and choice from the student's perspective and through a sociological lens. The monograph offers institutions helpful advice and information on how to broaden access to higher education by focusing on the inequities that exist in society in terms of academic preparation and aspirations and how schools (K–12 and higher education) can combat these inequities. This approach to the topic of college choice is necessary and important and all too easily lost in the search for ways to improve the institutional bottom line. This monograph is about college choice that focuses on how to provide access to college for a broader array of students than currently served and how to provide more equity to those who seek a college education. It also speaks to how institutions can better assist students in identifying colleges best suited to their needs and aspirations, thus expanding the range of institutions and institutional types students might consider in their search. One of this monograph's most valuable contributions is the review of college preparation programs and their effectiveness in increasing aspirations to go to college as well as expanding prospective students' understanding of the choices available to them in higher education. This review further takes into consideration the need for greater coordination and cooperation between the K–12 system and postsecondary institutions to improve the college choice process for all students.

The monograph is written for practitioners, graduate students, faculty, and researchers in higher education. It serves as an excellent companion piece to Marybeth Walpole's recent monograph (2007) on students who are economically and educationally disadvantaged. Both monographs grapple with the issues of college choice and access from complementary perspectives to offer a clear picture of how to better reach students who have historically been excluded from higher education. This subject is important because many believe that access to higher education in the United States is universal, that anyone and everyone can attend college. But although access to college has improved in some sectors of society, it has not improved for all. In 2005, more than 70 percent of individuals over the age of 24 in the highest income quartile earned a baccalaureate degree, while only 10 percent of those from the lowest income quartile earned one (Postsecondary Education Opportunity, 2008). Further, the disproportionate representation of low-income and minority students in community colleges and other nonselective institutions demonstrates a limited understanding of the full array of institutional options available. This monograph explores the literature on how to increase the number and types of students who aspire to earn a college degree, it provides information on how to help students expand their search options, and it offers ways to help students chose the right college. Improving the college choice process for a wider array of students is a bottom line worthy of institutional attention, focus, and resources.

Lisa E. Wolf-Wendel
Series Editor

Acknowledgments

Several individuals contributed to the completion of this monograph. Many thanks to Lisa Wolf-Wendel for her feedback and encouragement throughout the process and to the anonymous reviewers, whose comments shaped and refined the monograph. Natalie Brown's amazing literature search skills allowed me to churn through an extensive and complex body of literature in a short period of time. And I could not have completed this task without the patience, love, and support of Bill Biddle and Chase Bergerson. Thanks, guys.

Published online in Wiley InterScience
(www.interscience.wiley.com) • DOI: 10.1002/aehe.3504

Introduction to College Choice

C OLLEGE CHOICE HAS BEEN A TOPIC of investigation for many
years. Since the 1990 publication of Michael Paulsen's ASHE-ERIC
Higher Education Report on student enrollment behaviors, hundreds of pub-
lications have explored the processes through which students determine
whether and where to go to college and the factors that influence these
processes. This monograph reviews twenty years of literature on college choice,
building on Paulsen's work and illuminating new directions the research has
taken since 1990. Of particular note is the growing emphasis on the fact that
students of color and students from lower socioeconomic backgrounds attend
college at lower rates than white middle- and upper-class students. This focus on
the stratification of higher education in the United States is perhaps the most
notable aspect of the research reviewed in this monograph. Further, the pre-
dominance of quantitative methods for examining issues of college choice is
evident in the research of the last twenty years. Although this focus has allowed
for greater specification of variables that contribute to the choice process, there
is a clear need for additional qualitative work to further illuminate how and
why those variables affect students' postsecondary decisions.

Understanding college choice has potential implications for practice, policy, and research. Increasing competition for students among higher education institutions necessitates an understanding of the processes they use not
only to make institutional selections but also to decide whether to attend college at all. With cuts in institutional budgets as a result of the current economic recession, the need to target marketing and recruitment efforts is
growing. Increasing diversity in higher education necessitates developing the

ability to better serve a wider variety of students. Finally, in an era where many have declared that the United States has "moved beyond race," it is necessary to understand and resolve the persistent lack of representation of students of color and lower socioeconomic students in higher education.

This monograph examines college choice literature from the last two decades, identifying trends and patterns in the literature as well as in students' college choice processes. The monograph is organized in six sections: research trends since the publication of Paulsen's (1990) monograph; comprehensive models of college choice, emphasizing Hossler and Gallagher's three-stage model (1987) and introducing lenses through which the process is viewed; studies exploring the role of socioeconomic status in the college choice process; research examining the barriers and challenges to enrolling in higher education for students of color; literature related to college preparation programs designed to increase the participation of underserved students in higher education; and the implications and recommendations that follow a review of this research. Throughout, the monograph pays attention to enhancing the college choice processes of specific student populations.

College Access Versus College Choice

An examination of the processes students use to decide whether and where to go to college must differentiate between the concepts of college access and college choice. Much of the research presented in this monograph focuses on the choice process, the process through which students decide whether and where to go to college. Generally, this literature assumes that students who engage in the choice process have access to college. What is clear from many of the studies included in this volume is that access to higher education is not equitable, thus rendering theories of college choice only partially useful in understanding how students arrive at the decisions of whether to go to college and which institutions to attend. Considering issues of access complicates the study of college choice, but it is necessary to rethink our approaches to the college choice process with this issue in mind.

This monograph begins to unpack the complexity of the college choice process in an environment where equitable access to higher education is not available to every student by examining the precollege factors that play into students' access to college as well as the implications of policies intended to address issues of equity. The intent behind this effort is to generate a more holistic view of the processes students engage in when making decisions about postsecondary education. To do so, the monograph devotes specific attention to issues of access *and* choice for students of color and students from low socioeconomic backgrounds. This focus is grounded in the trend in the research since 1990 to further a better understanding of the college-going processes and behaviors of students from populations that are underrepresented in higher education.

Historical Perspectives on College Choice

To contextualize the literature published over the last twenty years, it is necessary to summarize briefly college choice research leading up to 1990. This description of the literature is not comprehensive, and readers who are interested in a deeper explication of the earlier research are encouraged to read Paulsen's ASHE-ERIC Higher Education Report (1990), which provides a detailed review of research produced in the 1970s and 1980s. The historical context presented here draws from Paulsen's work as well as specific significant studies cited in Paulsen's review.

Historically, the college choice process was framed by three perspectives: sociological, psychological, and economic (Paulsen, 1990). The sociological perspective focused on college choice as part of the status attainment process, with emphasis on individual background factors that influence the decision of whether and where to go to college. Background factors include race and ethnicity (Manski and Wise, 1983), family income (St. John, 1990), parent education (Manski and Wise, 1983), peer groups (Manski and Wise, 1983), school contexts (Alwin and Otto, 1977; Lee and Ekstrom, 1987), parental expectations (Attinasi, 1989; Litten and Hall, 1989), student and parent educational aspirations (Borus and Carpenter, 1984), academic achievement (St. John, 1990), and high school curriculum (Borus and Carpenter, 1984; Hearn, 1984). In studies framed by the sociological perspective, researchers found that student background characteristics have a significant impact on students' postsecondary choices, both in developing college predisposition and influencing their institutional choices.

The psychological perspective focused on the climate of the higher education environment and how perceptions of that climate influence students' institutional choices (Paulsen, 1990). Authors such as Tierney (1982), St. John (1990), and Manski and Wise (1983) found that institutional characteristics, including cost of tuition, room and board, location, curriculum, and financial aid availability, play into the psychological aspect of a college decision. The psychological dimension of the decision is driven by the interaction between student and institutional characteristics. For example, the authors cited above found that lower-income students find that factors related to cost and financial aid may outweigh curricular offerings as they make institutional choice decisions.

The economic perspective constructed the college choice process as an investment decision in which students weigh the costs and benefits of attending college and make choices based on their evaluation of the economic benefits of a postsecondary education (Paulsen, 1990). Factors that are taken into consideration in this decision process include the real financial cost of attending, the amount of financial aid available, and the forgone earnings from a decision to attend college. Students' perceptions of the return on their investment also shape the economic aspect of the decision. Historically, economic-based research argued that students are more likely to enroll in college when the perceived return on the investment is greater than the cumulative costs (Kodde and Ritzen, 1988). Additional research on the economics of the college choice decision noted students' price sensitivity; they are less likely to enroll when college costs increase or financial aid decreases (Leslie and Brinkman, 1987). Price sensitivity to both increases in tuition and decreases in grant aid is accentuated for students from lower socioeconomic backgrounds and students of color (St. John and Noell, 1989).

The 1980s brought a focus on developing comprehensive models to explain students' college choice processes. Chapman's causal model of college choice (1981) was based on factors that affected students' choice of which institution to attend. The model demonstrated how student characteristics (aspirations, socioeconomic status, academic ability, and achievement) and external factors (influential others, institutional characteristics, and institutional communication with students) interacted with students' expectations of the college experience to determine both which institutions students would apply to and their enrollment decisions. The model was explicitly developed to "assist college administrators responsible for recruitment policy to identify the pressures and influences they need to consider in developing institutional recruiting policy" (Chapman, 1981, p. 490). Chapman argued that understanding this complicated process would guide institutional efforts to communicate with students through the recruitment process.

Building on Chapman's model (1981), Litten (1982) examined how the process of institutional choice differs for students from different racial and ethnic groups, gender, academic ability, parent education, and geographic location. He found differences in the timing of the choice process, how college information was obtained, and parents' role in the planning process. These findings led Litten to argue that a "fully developed model of college choice" (p. 400) must recognize the main components of the process to be effective in assisting administrators responsible for recruitment develop optimal recruitment strategies. Litten also called on future researchers to examine ways that student attributes might contribute to the choice process of an increasingly diverse college-going population.

Chapman's and Litten's models illuminate students' institutional choice processes. Kotler and Fox's model (1985) incorporated the decision of *whether* to go to college by adding two stages to the enrollment decision steps: the consideration of alternative options such as work, military service, or higher education, and "product form alternatives" (p. 205) that included choices between public or private and large or small institutions. From here, models began to describe the entire process of college and institutional choice (Chapman and Jackson, 1987; Davis–Van Atta and Carrier, 1986), developing a series of steps or stages through which students progress from deciding whether to enter postsecondary education to their specific enrollment decisions.

The most widely cited model for understanding the comprehensive college choice process was created by Hossler and Gallagher (1987). Developed through a survey of research, the model identified three phases of the college choice process: (1) predisposition of students to attend college based on influences such as socioeconomic status, parental involvement, peers, interactions with higher education institutions, significant others, high school involvement, and the relative value placed on attending college; (2) search, in which higher education institutions supply potential students with information to assist in the decision process and students use this information to determine choice sets; and, (3) choice, in which students select an institution and complete the enrollment process.

Hossler and Gallagher's model of college choice (1987) is well known and has provided the foundation for subsequent research examining the college choice processes of a wide variety of students. For example, Hurtado, Inkelas, Briggs, and Rhee (1997) used the model to better understand the choice processes and behaviors of students of color in the National Educational Longitudinal Study database. More recently, Teranishi and others (2004) examined the college choice process of Asian Pacific American students. They found that students from different ethnic groups in that population used college choice factors in different ways and that the influence of Hossler and Gallagher's model varied among these students. These studies reflect a consistent trend in the literature after 1990, in which authors began to examine the experiences of students from different backgrounds with a more critical eye. In a move away from the development of comprehensive models, researchers began to question why higher education in the United States continues to be stratified by social class, race, and ethnicity. This move represents a refocusing of the research from issues of choice to issues of access. The content of this monograph is guided by this refocusing of the field.

Intended Audience

This monograph's focus on how students make postsecondary choices and the programs that support and enhance these choices has broad appeal to those who work in higher education. For teaching faculty, the monograph provides an extensive review of literature on which to base teaching efforts in the area of college choice and preparation. Students in higher education programs, in particular programs emphasizing student affairs, will find in the monograph numerous resources for their future studies and their practice. The monograph also outlines directions for future research that graduate students and research faculty can undertake.

Although the monograph is a resource for faculty and students, it also has the potential to inform professional practice. For professionals working to understand how students experience the college choice process, the monograph develops links between theory and practice. With these readers in mind, the literature is presented in a way that emphasizes the important connections between conceptual understandings and the world of practical application. The focus on equity and access woven throughout the monograph will appeal to those who seek a more critical approach to the literature and the issue of college choice. Ideas for improving practice are relevant both to professionals working in higher education environments and those who interact with students in K–12 systems, encouraging more cooperation between these two environments to increase access to higher education for all students who aspire to it.

Implications for policymakers are also presented. The last twenty years have seen an increase in studies that focus on how state and federal policies influence access to higher education for various groups. Policies in the areas of admissions, federal and state funding of higher education, and the availability and composition of federal and state financial aid all have an impact on students' perceptions of and enrollment in higher education institutions. This research makes clear that providing equitable access to higher education is not simply an institutional or individual student issue, but one that policy must address as well.

Limitations

The scope of the literature on college choice is extensive, and this monograph attempts to present a thorough review of this vast body of research. What this review covers has limitations, however. First, the literature presented pertains largely to traditional-aged college students, 18- to 24-year-olds in the process of deciding whether and where to attend college. The scant body of research on adult learners tends to focus on their experiences once they are in the college environment (see, for example, Hensley and Kinser, 2001; Sissel, Hansman, and Kasworm, 2001) and not the processes through which they decide to go to college, and for that reason, it is not included here. Additionally, though an effort was made to include literature pertaining directly to community college choice processes, this review is not able to explicate the choice processes of students making this specific institutional choice. Some literature about community colleges is included in the review as it contributes to the areas of focus described above. Military options and opportunities (such as the GI bill) are also not specified in this review. Finally, choice processes regarding for-profit and distance education opportunities are not included in the review, as the literature in these areas is particularly scant. Clearly, further research in these areas is needed to paint a more complete picture of the processes through which students decide whether and where to go to college.

Organization of the Monograph

This monograph builds on research reviewed in Paulsen's monograph on college student enrollment behaviors (1990), focusing on how researchers have enhanced our understanding of the college choice process in the last two decades. The next chapter, "Current Trends in College Choice Research," focuses on where the research on college choice has gone since 1989. The field's trend toward attempting to better understand the experiences of students from populations underrepresented in higher education, the trend away from developing comprehensive models of choice, and the focus on precollege environments, dispositions, and backgrounds that influence the choice process are highlighted. Finally, it discusses the trend toward policy analysis and development to enhance the college-going process for students from diverse backgrounds.

"College Choice as a Comprehensive Process" revisits Hossler and Gallagher's three-stage model of college choice (1987) and explores its expansion and critique in recent studies. Additionally, newer research related to college choice as a comprehensive process is presented. This research moves away from the idea of developing a general model of choice applied to all students and emphasizes the importance of recognizing the distinct backgrounds and experiences of an increasingly diverse college-going population. Bourdieu's concepts of habitus, capital, and field (1977, 1987, 1993) are introduced as frames for understanding how background characteristics play into college choice processes. Cultural wealth (Villalpando and Solorzano, 2005) is also explicated as a means for understanding the experiences of students as they move through the college choice process. Finally, the chapter introduces several models of college choice emerging in the last decade, some of which examine the role of context in the choice process, and addresses the ways these contexts shape students' postsecondary enrollment decisions.

"College Choice for Lower-Socioeconomic Students" explores the impact of individual and family background factors on the college choice process. Of particular importance in this chapter is the growing gap among the aspirations, expectations, and enrollment of lower-socioeconomic students. This chapter emphasizes the use of Bourdieu's constructs (1977, 1987, 1993) to illuminate the role family background plays in students' access to and choices regarding postsecondary education. "College Choice Processes for Students of Color" explores the continuing stratification of higher education institutions by race and ethnicity, examining literature that illuminates several explanations for this stratification. The chapter calls for the need to move beyond "deficit thinking" (Solorzano and Ornelas, 2004) and its negative impact on the enrollment of underrepresented students in higher education. Research on the specific barriers encountered by students of color and information on how students navigate those barriers are presented.

"College Preparation Programs" introduces seven college preparation programs, briefly assessing their structure compared with Corwin, Colyar, and Tierney's framework (2005) for essential college preparation program components. Program structures are also related to the research reviewed in previous chapters to provide links between theory and practice. The final chapter, "Implications and Recommendations for Practice, Policy, and Research," develops these links more specifically, first summarizing the recommendations for practice, policy, and research from Paulsen's monograph (1990) and then grounding implications and recommendations for research, practice, and policy in the literature presented in the first five chapters.

A foundational assumption guiding the research for and writing of this monograph is that it is the responsibility of those working in and around higher education institutions and policymaking bodies to determine ways to increase access to the wide range of postsecondary opportunities for *every* student who aspires to a college education. Teaching, research, practice, and policy in the area of college choice should be guided by the goal of creating equitable environments to which all students have access and in which all students can reach their potential.

Current Trends in College Choice Research

PAULSEN'S REVIEW OF RESEARCH on college choice (1990) included references to more than two hundred studies, primarily from the 1970s and 1980s. Paulsen's monograph focused on the enrollment management field, with the intent of expanding professionals' understanding of how and why students choose higher education generally and various institutions specifically. The literature reviewed by Paulsen supported this emphasis in its focus on the factors that influence college choice decisions, the processes students use to make those decisions, and the social, psychological, and economic explanations for the impact of these factors and processes.

In the twenty years since the publication of Paulsen's work, the focus of much of the college choice research has shifted to one of access and equity. Researchers, armed with a basic understanding of the processes and characteristics that play into students' postsecondary plans, have made a clear call for a deeper understanding of the factors that contribute to the continued stratification in American higher education. This emphasis on equity is the umbrella under which three other trends sit. The first is a trend away from comprehensive college choice models. This movement reflects an understanding across the field that the college-going population in the United States is growing increasingly diverse, complicating the ability of any model to define or describe the myriad experiences students have in this process. The second area of focus in the more recent literature is preparation for college. Many researchers have examined college preparation programs as well as community and school characteristics that affect students' preparation for college. Within this research is a specific emphasis on access to information and academic preparation for college. The final major trend in the literature of the last twenty years is a focus on policy. Although Paulsen's monograph was written primarily for institutional enrollment managers, current college choice research moves beyond the institution to state and federal policies, with calls for examinations of how such policies help or hinder students' access to the postsecondary environment. This chapter focuses on each of these areas as a means of introducing the field of college choice today.

Access and Equity in College Choice

Recent reports from the National Center for Education Statistics (NCES) (Radford, Tasoff, and Weko, 2009) indicate that higher education in the United States is stratified by race and social class. Table 1, showing the percentage of recent high school graduates from different racial and ethnic groups enrolled in four-year institutions, illustrates the disproportionate representation of white students in four-year institutions. Clearly, white students are overrepresented compared with recent high school graduates of color in these institutions. In two-year institutions, although students of color have greater representation than in four-year institutions, white students make up the majority of enrolled students: 63.4 percent of enrolled students are white, 12.2 percent are black, 14.5 percent are Hispanic, 4.9 percent are Asian, and the

TABLE 1
Percent of 2003–2004 Beginning Postsecondary Students by Race

Race/Ethnicity	Public Four-Year Institutions	Private (Not-for-Profit) Four-Year Institutions
White	70.1	73.2
Black	8.4	8.7
Hispanic	6.4	5.2
Asian	6.4	5.2
Other	5.4	3.9

Source: Adapted from Radford, Tasoff, and Weko, National Center for Education Statistics Issue Tables, 2009, p. 186.

remaining 4.9 percent are "other." When it comes to income level, students from high- and high-middle-income households are more highly represented than those from lower-income households, particularly in private four-year institutions, where they make up nearly 60 percent of enrolled students (Radford, Tasoff, and Weko, 2009). At the other end of the spectrum, students from the lowest-income households make up only 17 percent of postsecondary students.

Another measure of socioeconomic status, parent education, also appears to affect college enrollment. According to the NCES, only 14.7 percent of students enrolled in private four-year institutions have parents who did not attend a postsecondary institution themselves. Conversely, students whose parents have graduate degrees make up 36 percent of the population enrolled in this type of institution. These data illustrate the ongoing stratification of the postsecondary environment by race, ethnicity, and social class. This stratification has drawn the attention of researchers who are interested in exploring the different experiences of students of color (see, for example, Azmitia and Cooper, 2001; Freeman, 1997, 1999; Kao and Thompson, 2003; Perna, 2000) and students from lower socioeconomic backgrounds (for example, Cabrera and LaNasa, 2001; McDonough, 1997; Terenzini, Cabrera, and Bernal, 2001; Walpole, 2003) as they engage in the college choice process.

An overview of the literature related to students of color and students from low socioeconomic backgrounds (details regarding the experiences of these two groups of students are addressed in later chapters) highlights a number of areas of concern. First, it is apparent that students of color and students from lower socioeconomic backgrounds are less prepared for higher education than white middle- and upper-class students. Adelman (2006) noted that students of color have less access to higher-level math courses in their high schools and that students from lower socioeconomic backgrounds access such courses at lower rates than middle- and upper-class students. Solorzano and Ornelas (2004) also found that schools with lower resources, largely populated by students of color, offer fewer advanced placement courses, known for enhancing the college enrollment of students who take them. The current tax-based funding structure of public education in the United States virtually guarantees a higher-quality education to students who live in higher socioeconomic neighborhoods.

Perna's individual work (2005b) and joint efforts (Perna, Steele, Woda, and Hibbert, 2005) on academic preparation emphasized the role of policy in shaping academic opportunities both at the state and national levels.

Another issue facing students of color and students of lower socioeconomic status relates to the economic approach to college choice; these students face particular uncertainties about the payoffs of attending college that strongly influence whether and where they decide to attend. Several authors (Cooper and others, 1995; Hanson, 1994; Mickelson, 1990; Pitre, 2006a) focused on the gap between the aspirations and achievement of students of color and lower socioeconomic students. One finding of this line of research was the lack of access to role models who came from similar backgrounds and for whom college provided increased economic opportunity. Many students had aspirations of attending college early on, but as they were exposed to others in their community for whom higher education did not make a significant economic difference, their aspirations declined. For others, lack of academic preparation and limited access to information about college played a role in their declining aspirations. All of these factors played into students' inability to accurately weigh the costs and benefits of attending college.

Information is a significant element of the college choice process. Comprehensive models such as Hossler and Gallagher's framework (1987) emphasize students' process of collecting and assessing various types of information about postsecondary institutions. It is clear from the research, however, that for students of color and lower socioeconomic students, information about college options is hard to come by. Families with limited personal experiences with higher education (Grodsky and Jones, 2007, Ikenberry and Hartle, 1998), lack of contact with high school counselors (Gonzalez, Stoner, and Jovel, 2003), peers who are not necessarily college bound (Perez and McDonough, 2008), and high schools with low levels of resources for college guidance (Perna and others, 2008) all contribute to a lower understanding of postsecondary opportunities, the costs of attending, and the resources available to aid in funding an education. Faced with myriad choices, complicated forms, and unfamiliar terms and acronyms, it is no wonder that students of color and students from lower socioeconomic backgrounds choose not to go to college.

All these findings make the utility of comprehensive college choice models problematic. In particular, they debunk a fundamental assumption of these models—that students have equal access to higher education. It is clear from the work examining the experiences of students of color and of lower socioeconomic status that not everyone faces the college choice process armed with the same tools and opportunities. Overwhelmingly, researchers in the last twenty years attempted to shed light on the many factors that potentially complicate students' access to postsecondary education. This monograph reiterates the need to explore these issues further, as the research reveals numerous unanswered questions about why higher education in the United States continues to be most consistently accessed by white middle- and upper-class students.

Utility of Comprehensive College Choice Models in the Twenty-First Century

The last two decades of college choice research have seen a growing emphasis on the continued stratification of higher education in the United States. The NCES (U.S. Department of Education, 2005) reported that although participation in postsecondary education had increased for all racial and ethnic groups from 1974 to 2003, increases in participation for whites were larger than for blacks and Hispanics, indicating an achievement gap between these groups. Research also found that differences in enrollment exist for students from lower socioeconomic backgrounds (see, for example, Beattie, 2002; Breen and Goldthorpe, 1997; Ellwood and Kane, 2000; Hanson, 1994) and attempted to explain these differences. From the volume of published research exploring these concerns, it is clear that the field is moving away from the notion of developing comprehensive explanatory models to a focus on access to higher education for students from a wide range of backgrounds.

The work of several scholars found that students of color engage in a search process that differs from that of white students. For example, Teranishi and others (2004) found that both ethnicity in Asian Pacific Americans and socioeconomic status had an effect on how students experienced the college choice process. Specific ethnic groups in the study population experienced significant differences in the institutional choice part of the process, with some groups heavily represented in more selective institutions and others in less selective ones. Further, socioeconomic status had a differential impact on the choice processes of students from various ethnic groups, with higher degrees of variation in college attendance by socioeconomic status in Chinese students and lower degrees of variation in the Southeast Asian and Korean student groups. Ultimately, Teranishi and others reported, "APA students from different ethnic backgrounds were not always similar in their college-choice processes nor were APA sub-populations similar in the factors that impacted their eventual college destinations" (p. 546). This finding indicates that comprehensive college choice models may not adequately predict or explain the college choice processes of students from a variety of backgrounds.

Another example of research that questions the utility of comprehensive college choice models is Hurtado, Inkelas, Briggs, and Rhee's study (1997) of the barriers faced by students of color as they move toward postsecondary education. Using data from the National Education Longitudinal Study for 1988–1992, these authors found that students of colors' experiences with college preparation, application, and enrollment were different from those of white students. The authors posited that significant differences in academic achievement led to gaps in the types of information to which students had access, which then influenced the range of postsecondary options available to them. The authors noted that this domino effect leads to a loss of talent evident in the divergent futures (p. 62) of these students over time. The authors concluded that comprehensive college choice models had a value in framing their study but that "more precise models of the predisposition phase [are necessary] to understand the vast differences in student preparation for college among racial/ethnic groups" (p. 64). This conclusion provides further evidence against the utility of comprehensive models, which Freeman echoes (1997, 1999).

Freeman (1997, 1999) also argued for a reconceptualization of comprehensive college choice models as a result of her studies of African American students' college choice experiences. Noting that postcollege job expectations and the aspiration-attainment gap are particularly salient features of African Americans' postsecondary education choice processes, Freeman (1999) argued that existing college choice models fail to consider the context in which particular factors become significant for students. Moreover, Freeman (1997) noted that "defin[ing] the problem and develop[ing] the solutions based on models that are applicable to the majority population" (p. 548) contribute to African Americans' continued marginalization and lack of participation in higher education.

The work of early researchers who focused on the development of comprehensive college choice models represents an essential contribution to the field. Models developed by Chapman (1981), Litten (1982), Kotler and Fox, (1985), Chapman and Jackson (1987), Davis–Van Atta and Carrier (1986), and Hossler and Gallagher (1987) framed ongoing discussion and research around the topic of college choice. Of particular note is the contribution these models made to the ability of future researchers to define and measure variables that significantly affect the processes students use to decide whether and where to go to college. Examining the influence of a wide range of variables in the process led the field to its current focus on equity, as we have observed and begun to explain how variations in the influence of these factors apply to the experiences of students from diverse backgrounds. Although these models will undoubtedly continue to influence how the field frames college choice as well as the particular variables of interest to researchers, it is also important for the field to continue to generate research that examines the experiences of students from groups that have been traditionally underserved in higher education. The issue of access to postsecondary education for students of color and lower socioeconomic status students is addressed in the remaining chapters of the monograph.

Preparation for College

Much of the literature in the last twenty years has emphasized the importance of preparing students for college. Two strands of research make up this emphasis: a focus on programs specifically intended to provide students with the skills, knowledge, and information needed to engage in the college choice process and a consideration of the differential experiences of students' high school experiences in terms of preparing them for the postsecondary environment. College preparation programs take many forms. Given the issues of access discussed earlier, many are intended to provide students from underrepresented populations in higher education with knowledge and information necessary to make decisions about attending college. Other programs focus on skill development through study skills courses, college preparation courses, and counseling intended to develop decision-making skills. Other programs are intended for students who are already interested in postsecondary education, enhancing their preexisting skills through structured experiences. Many programs have financial components intended to help ease the monetary burden of college attendance. The research on what makes a college preparation program effective is reviewed in detail in "College Preparation Programs" later in this volume. In short, however, the essential components of college preparation programs (Corwin, Colyar, and Tierney, 2005) include relationships with others that recognize and build on the cultural assets of the students to promote self-efficacy, academic preparation for college through development of course taking and study skills, information about higher education generally, and information about and access to financial support.

In addition to illuminating the growing number of programs intended to improve the college-going rates of various student populations, recent research also explores how students' experiences in high school shape their college choice processes. Pitre's study of black and white college students (2006a) found that when black students perceived that their high school courses were not preparing them for college, their aspirations to a postsecondary education decreased. When this finding is taken with Solorzano and Ornelas's argument (2004) that students of color attend high schools with fewer college preparatory courses, the implication is clear: students who are not being prepared for college are less likely to enroll in college. In addition to inequities in academic preparation, Gonzales, Stoner, and Jovel (2003) argued that Latinas had less access to high school personnel who could provide them with information about higher education. This finding was supported by the research of Perna and others (2008), who found that schools with fewer financial resources had limited infrastructure in the form of counseling and information to aid students in exploring postsecondary options.

The increased focus on college preparation in the last twenty years recognizes the complex environment in which students make postsecondary decisions. At the forefront of this emphasis is an illustration of the inequities in

K–12 schooling experiences that affect the ability of students in low-resource schools, predominantly students of color and low socioeconomic status, to engage in the college choice process. Following the trend away from comprehensive models of college choice, this research calls for practitioners and policymakers to attend to resolving identified inequities and to develop programs to fill the gaps in the college preparation of students whose educational environments do not support their postsecondary aspirations.

Increased Policy Focus

Paulsen's monograph (1990) was directed largely at institutional enrollment management efforts, including the processes of planning for enrollment, marketing institutions to students, and recruiting students. Since then, researchers have increasingly emphasized the role of state, federal, and institutional policies in influencing students' decisions about whether and where to attend college. Much of this research is driven by the growing awareness of the severe underrepresentation of students of color and lower socioeconomic status in higher education institutions, a situation, many argue, that institutions lack the ability to resolve.

Studies analyzing, evaluating, and recommending policies to support students' enrollment in postsecondary education focus primarily on state and federal levels, largely examining how financial aid influences decisions about whether and where to attend college. At the forefront of policy work are Heller (1997, 1999), Perna, Steele, Woda, and Hibbert (2005), and Perna and Titus (2005), all of whom examined how state and federal policies affect the stratification of higher education by race, ethnicity, and social class. Additionally, Lillis (2008) and St. John (1994) examined the role of financial aid policies in the enrollment of students from different social class backgrounds. All of these authors argued that the trend in the last three decades toward an increasing reliance on loans to fund higher education works against students of color and low socioeconomic status who aspire to postsecondary education. Whether because of debt aversion, the ambiguity around whether investment in a college education will offer sufficient returns, or a lack of information about the availability of financial aid, students of color and lower socioeconomic status are less likely to take out loans to finance a college education. Federal and state policies that move away from need-based grants and scholarships exacerbate the continued stratification of higher education in the United States. The research in the policy arena calls for continued examination of the barriers such policies build for underrepresented student populations and contributes to the overall focus in the last two decades on issues of access and equity in the college choice process.

Chapter Summary

The shifting focus from enrollment management to understanding issues of access and equity related to the college choice process has shaped the research of the last twenty years. Building on the knowledge developed in the 1970s and 1980s, researchers refined variables, tested theories, and began to learn how factors that play into students' lives long before college enrollment becomes a pressing issue shape their educational aspirations and eventual choices. This work shaped the trends described earlier—focus on equity and access, move away from comprehensive models, attention to college preparation, and increased policy focus—each of which addresses in some way the different experiences underrepresented groups have throughout the educational process and contributes to the conversation about how college choice processes can be made more equitable for these students. To further develop this conversation, the next chapter reviews the predominant comprehensive college choice models, presents research addressing the utility of these models in the current educational environment, and illuminates several models currently being used by researchers to better understand the college choice process.

College Choice as a Comprehensive Process

THE PROCESS OF CHOOSING whether and where to attend college is frequently viewed as a comprehensive process in which students realize their college-going aspirations through the use of several steps leading to enrollment. Henrickson (2002, p. 403) defined "process models" as those that "capture elements of potential students, institutional characteristics, and the college application process" and that view the college choice process as developmental (see, for example, Chapman, 1981; Litten, 1982; and Hossler and Gallagher, 1987). Characteristic of these models is the ability to illustrate the interactions among individual students, institutional characteristics, and external factors as students make postsecondary plans (Henrickson, 2002). It is widely agreed that process models are robust, as they paint a picture of interactions over time and provide researchers with numerous process points and variables for further research (Cabrera and LaNasa, 2000; Henrickson, 2002; Jackson, 1986; Perna, 2006; Teranishi and others, 2004).

Perhaps the most widely cited and used process model is Hossler and Gallagher's three-stage model (1987), which is based on their synthesis of literature about college choice. Researchers have studied the predisposition phase of the model (Bouse and Hossler, 1991; Brooks, 2003; Hossler and Stage, 1992; Lillard and Gerner, 1999), application processes (Hearn, 1991; Leslie and Brinkman, 1987; Nora, 2004; Smith, 2007), and institutional factors (DesJardins, Ahlburg, and McCall, 2006; Hartley and Morphew, 2008; Sanders, 1990; Smith, 2007; Stewart and Post, 1990) that play into the choice process. Process models have provided a foundation for ongoing college choice research. This chapter begins with a detailed explication of Hossler and Gallagher's model and then moves into a review of additional research that builds on, expands, and critiques this model. This review includes brief descriptions of new college choice models. It then considers two lenses that are gaining in popularity for examining the college choice process: Bourdieu's theory of social reproduction (1977, 1987, 1993) and the concept of cultural wealth (Villalpando and Solorzano, 2005). Both frameworks allow researchers to examine the nuances of the college choice process for underrepresented student populations.

Hossler and Gallagher's College Choice Model

Hossler and Gallagher's model (1987) comprises three phases through which students progress as they move from educational aspirations to college enrollment. Like Chapman's and Litten's models, Hossler and Gallagher's model is considered developmental (Henrickson, 2002) in that each stage is associated with particular "cognitive and affective outcomes" (Cabrera and LaNasa, 2000, p. 5) that ultimately lead to enrollment in college. Also associated with the developmental nature of Hossler and Gallagher's model is the tendency of researchers to assign age ranges to each stage. For example, Cabrera and LaNasa suggested that students begin the process in seventh grade and complete it when they enroll in a higher education institution at the end of twelfth grade (p. 6). A detailed description of the model's stages follows.

Predisposition

The first stage of Hossler and Gallagher's model is *predisposition*, which involves the development of students' college aspirations and expectations. Numerous factors influence students' college predisposition, including family socioeconomic status, parental involvement, peers, high school teachers and counselors, interactions with higher education institutions, high school involvement, and the relative value placed on attending college (Perna and Titus, 2004). Parental influences have been found to be among the highest predictors of a student's enrollment in college (Hossler, Schmit, and Vesper, 1999; Hamrick and Stage, 1995, 2000, 2004). Hossler, Schmit, and Vesper (1999) differentiate between parental encouragement and parental support, with encouragement defined as conversations between students and their parents about parental expectations and aspirations and support defined more behaviorally as saving for college, visiting higher education campuses with students, and participating in financial aid workshops (p. 24). Other researchers have found that parental involvement in a student's education (Perna and Titus, 2005; Ramirez, 2001; Rowan-Kenyon, Bell, and Perna, 2008; Tierney, 2002) and level of parents' education (Conley, 2001; Ellwood and Kane, 2000; Hallinan, 2000; Hossler and Stage, 1992) are also significant predictors of college attendance. Another family factor that affects predisposition and eventual enrollment in college is socioeconomic status. For many students who aspire to a postsecondary education, financial concerns present a barrier to the fulfillment of those aspirations (Lillis, 2008; McPherson and Shapiro, 1991). Several studies show that students from low socioeconomic backgrounds and students of color are more sensitive to increases in price and the type and availability of financial aid, both as they initially consider postsecondary education and as they weigh the options as they near the choice phase of the process (Callendar and Jackson, 2008; Dynarski, 2002, 2003; Grodsky and Jones, 2007).

Although family variables clearly shape the predisposition phase of the choice process, significant others such as peers, teachers, and counselors also influence students' perceptions of and aspirations for postsecondary education. Supportive teachers and counselors (McDonough, Korn, and Yamasaki, 1997; Muhammad, 2008; Rosenbaum, Miller, and Krei, 1996) and a peer group that also aspires to a college education (Brooks, 2003; Gibson, Gandara, and Koyama, 2004; Goddard, 2003; Perez and McDonough, 2008) increase students' predisposition toward college.

Individual factors also influence college predisposition. Students whose academic achievement is high are more likely to aspire to a college education (Gardner, Ritblatt, and Beatty, 2000; Hossler, Schmit, and Vesper, 1999). Further, a student's understanding of college and his or her ability to access information about higher education also play into the predisposition phase (Hossler, Schmit, and Vesper, 1999; Morgan, 2002). Many variables shape predisposition, which Cabrera and LaNasa (2000) argued takes place during the seventh through ninth grades. It is clear, however, that important elements of predisposition are active long before students reach early adolescence. Frequently students and parents reported that they simply "assumed" that college would follow high school (see, for example, Hossler, Schmit, and Vesper, 1999), indicating that predisposition is formed from the beginning of students' educational socialization. Although aspirations for a college education are an important factor in students' actual enrollment (Hossler, Schmit, and Vesper, 1999), they must be accompanied by actions that lead to the fulfillment of those hopes. These actions begin to emerge in the search stage of Hossler and Gallagher's model (1987).

Search

The second phase of Hossler and Gallagher's model (1987) is *search*, in which students form choice sets and determine which institutional characteristics are most important. This step involves learning more about themselves and the institutions in which they are interested. Students planning to attend college typically take entrance examinations like the ACT or SAT during the search phase, and their performance on these examinations further influences their choices. Choices are also determined by students' socioeconomic status, their parents' education, and the availability of financial support. The search phase of the college choice process generally occurs during the tenth through twelfth grades (Cabrera and LaNasa, 2000; Perna, 2006).

As in the predisposition phase, parental encouragement is a significant aspect of the search stage of Hossler and Gallagher's model. Hossler, Schmit, and Vesper (1999) noted the differences between parental influence and parental support in the search phase. Parents influence their children by sending signals about the choice process. Predisposition reflects parents' educational level as well as the educational attainment of students' siblings and extended family. Through direction setting, parents establish whether the child is going to college "long before high school" and what curricular choices in high school will set the course for this outcome (p. 63). Price and proximity are signals parents send to children that lay out expectations about where they can afford to send the child to college and how close to home the college should be. Finally, parents indicate to children their expectations regarding institutional quality. Related to this phase is the importance of "family traditions," which Dixon and Martin (1991) found influenced students' choice decisions. All of these forms of influence shape the choice set that students develop during the search phase.

Parental support, on the other hand, includes tangible activities such as saving for college, participating in college visits, sending students to summer camps, and assisting in filling out forms (Hossler, Schmit, and Vesper, 1999). Hossler, Schmit, and Vesper also suggested that parents' impact on the choice process begins to decrease during the search phase, with the strongest impact of their expectations on forming the predisposition and shaping the choice set, a finding supported by Galotti and Mark (1994).

Another area in which parents influence the search stage of the college choice process is in their knowledge and understanding of the costs of college and the availability of financial aid (Cabrera and LaNasa, 2000; DesJardins, Ahlburg, and McCall, 2006). Several studies noted the connection between parental background characteristics such as education and social class and their knowledge of financial aid programs (Grodsky and Jones, 2007; Ikenberry and Hartle, 1998; Paulsen and St. John, 2002). Lower-income families and families whose parents have lower education levels tend to overestimate the costs of college and underestimate the availability of and their eligibility for financial aid (Cabrera and LaNasa, 2000; Ikenberry and Hartle, 1998). Further, Flint (1997) found that parents' experiences of financing their own college educations shaped the strategies they used to fund their children's postsecondary educations. This intergenerational effect results in an advantage for students whose parents have higher levels of education. Overall, the search phase includes considerations of college costs and availability of aid. A number of authors expressed concern about students' and parents' general lack of awareness about college costs and the funding avenues available (Grodsky and Jones, 2007; Ikenberry and Hartle, 1998), indicating a need for information in these areas.

Information gathering is a central element of the search process (Hossler and Gallagher, 1987). Hossler, Schmit, and Vesper (1999) argued that three types of information-gathering techniques are used: attentive, active, and interactive. Based on earlier research by Schmit (1991), the authors defined attentive search as a passive interest in conversations and information about postsecondary options. In active search, students are seekers of information and conversation about available options. Finally, interactive searchers initiate discussions with family members, teachers, and counselors. This type of information gathering also includes initiating conversations with college representatives and requesting information from higher education institutions (Hossler, Schmit, and Vesper, 1999, p. 60). Hartley and Morphew (2008) recently noted that despite the increasing ability to access information electronically, print materials distributed to interested students by higher education institutions remain an important source of information in the search process.

Given the importance of information in the search process, several studies explored issues of access to information. McDonough's study of students' choice process (1997) found that students from higher socioeconomic backgrounds have greater access to and ability to locate information. These findings were supported by other authors (Hamrick and Hossler, 1996; McDonough, Antonio, Walpole, and Perez, 1998; Person and Rosenbaum, 2006). Further, McDonough, Korn, and Yamasaki (1997) found that students who used independent education consultants in the search process came from higher socioeconomic families with higher levels of social and cultural capital, had higher academic achievement rates, and were more likely to use high school personnel in the process than students who did not use independent education consultants as information sources. In response to this information gap, Cabrera and LaNasa (2000) suggested that high school resources, including teachers and counselors, are of particular importance for low-income, first-generation students.

The role of high school personnel in the college choice process is disputed. Hossler, Schmit, and Vesper (1999) noted that students relied on high school teachers and counselors more in the later phases. Johnson and Stewart (1991) found that black students were more likely to access information from high school counselors than whites and that assistance from counselors was sought more often than from teachers. Despite some argument (Cabrera and LaNasa, 2000; Plank and Jordan, 2001; Terenzini, Cabrera, and Bernal, 2001) that high school personnel can bridge the information gap for low-income students, other research has found that high school personnel have a limited role in students' postsecondary education selections (Freeman, 1997; Galotti and Mark, 1994; Stanton-Salazar and Dornbusch, 1995).

Several college preparation programs such as AVID, GEARUP, and Upward Bound focus on including increased interaction with high school teachers and counselors as a means of assisting lower socioeconomic and first-generation students and students of color to access information about post-secondary options (Cooper and others, 1995; Gandara, 2002; Grubb, Lara, and Valdez, 2002; Tierney and Jun, 2001). Overall, these studies report positive results from students' regular use of well-informed and student-centered high school personnel in information gathering, echoing Freeman's finding that actively engaged teachers and counselors in structured counseling situations enhance the college choice process of African American students.

Generally, Hossler and Gallagher's search stage is one in which students seek information and use it to develop initial institutional choice sets. Hossler, Schmit, and Vesper (1999) noted that although students' lists of important institutional characteristics are somewhat rudimentary at this stage, they begin to consider what is important to them in light of the influence felt from parental expectations. During this stage, students begin to move away from parents as primary information sources, relying more on peers and on materials and representatives from higher education institutions as they further define their choice sets. This phase also involves taking college entrance examinations and ultimately completing the application process for those institutions in the final choice set. By the middle of the senior year, students are ready to move to the final stage of the process, choice.

Choice

In the *choice* stage of Hossler and Gallagher's model, students use information to select an institution and complete the enrollment process. This stage occurs in the eleventh and twelfth grades (Cabrera and LaNasa, 2000; Perna, 2006). According to Hossler, Schmit, and Vesper (1999), institutional characteristics play an important role in the choice process. Cabrera and LaNasa (2000) also listed institutional factors among several that play into the final enrollment decision, including "parental encouragement, financial considerations, the student's high school academic resources, the student's educational and occupational aspirations, and, of course, the student's academic abilities" (p. 6). It follows that students' information-gathering capacity is also an essential element of choice as students collect the final inputs into their decisions. In terms of sources of information, the roles of parents and peers diminish during this phase, with institutions more directly influencing students' institutional choice decisions.

One area that gains importance as students make enrollment decisions is college cost and financial aid. Hossler, Schmit, and Vesper (1999) noted that students were not "interested" (p. 131) in these issues until the senior year, communicating to researchers before this time that paying for college was their parents' responsibility. A number of studies examined the role of financial aid in students' enrollment decisions (Dynarski, 2002, 2003; Lillis, 2008; St. John, 1994), and found that students do consider both cost and available aid in the search and choice process. In another angle, Avery and Hoxby's work (2004) uncovered the importance of students' perceptions of aid in the enrollment process. They found that how aid was labeled ("grant" versus "scholarship") made a difference in students' enrollment decisions. Studies examining the role of financial aid in enrollment decisions have both institutional and policy implications, as it is clear that college costs and aid do affect students' decisions (Callendar and Jackson, 2008; Heller, 1997, 1999; Hossler, 2000; Kim, 2004; Paulsen and St. John, 2002; Reay, Davies, David, and Ball, 2001), that type of aid matters (Dynarski, 2002; Ikenberry and Hartle, 1998; Perna and Titus, 2004), and that the impact is more deeply felt by students from lower socioeconomic backgrounds and students of color (Dynarski, 2003; Ikenberry and Hartle, 1998; Lillis, 2008; McPherson and Shapiro, 1998; Paulsen and St. John, 2002). Finally, studies also indicated that students of color and their families have less access to information about cost and financial aid, which negatively affects both their educational aspirations and their actual enrollment in higher education (Hao and Bonstead-Bruns, 1998; Post, 1990).

Economic approaches to the issue of college choice also emphasize the importance of price in students' enrollment decisions (Breen and Goldthorpe, 1997; Curs and Singell, 2002; DesJardins, Ahlburg, and McCall, 2006; Heller, 1999). Rational choice models suggest that students are able to weigh the costs and benefits of a college education and determine whether and where to attend based on their estimates of each (Hatcher, 1998; Hossler, Braxton, and Coopersmith, 1989). Perna (2000) proposed an expanded model of "college enrollment investment decisions" (p. 122) to explain differences in enrollment by race and ethnicity. By incorporating Bourdieu's concepts (1977) of social and cultural capital in the econometric approach, Perna revealed differences in the decision of whether to attend college in different racial and ethnic groups. Beattie (2002) also found differences in students' ability to accurately weigh the costs and benefits of higher education by race, class, and gender. Pitre's theory of reasoned action (2006b) in the college choice decision addressed concerns expressed by Perna and Beattie by accounting for students' behavioral intentions and attitudes and norms, all of which provide context for an individual's ability to rationally determine the costs and benefits of attending college.

Information about institutional characteristics is also essential to the choice stage of the process. Literature on the institutional choice process found that location (DesJardins, Dundar, and Hendel, 1999; Goenner and Pauls, 2006; Reay, Davies, David, and Ball, 2001; Stewart and Post, 1990), course and program offerings (DesJardins, Dundar, and Hendel, 1999; Johnson and Stewart, 1991; Sanders, 1990), reputation (Johnson and Stewart, 1991; McDonough, Antonio, Walpole, and Perez, 1998; Smith, 1990), sense of fit (Nora, 2004; Reay, Davies, David, and Ball, 2001; Smith, 2007), and social opportunities (Nora, 2004) are among the institutional factors that students weigh in their enrollment decisions. The importance of these factors appears to vary for students from different socioeconomic, racial, and ethnic backgrounds (McDonough, Antonio, Walpole, and Perez, 1998; Stewart and Post, 1990).

Parental encouragement and students' aspirations and expectations also affect enrollment decisions (Cabrera and LaNasa, 2000). Parental influence signals (Hossler, Schmit, and Vesper, 1999) shape students' institutional choice sets and further affect their enrollment decisions. Specifically, parental influence in areas of financial support and encouragement to attend particular institutions has some effect on students' choices (Dixon and Martin, 1991). Parental background factors also shape students' educational aspirations and expectations (Conley, 2001; Hofferth, Boisjoly, and Duncan, 1998; Lopez-Turley, Santos, and Ceja, 2007). Research supports the notion that aspirations and expectations play into students' enrollment decisions (Kao and Tienda, 1998; Reynolds and Pemberton, 2001; Solorzano, 1992), despite evidence of an aspiration-attainment gap among some groups of students (Hanson, 1994; Immerwahr, 2003; Mickelson, 1990; Morgan, 1996).

Students' academic achievement is an important factor in the choice phase of Hossler and Gallagher's model. Students with higher levels of academic achievement have more postsecondary options (Hurtado, Inkelas, Briggs, and Rhee, 1997; Teranishi, Allen, and Solorzano, 2004), have more access to information about higher education (Hurtado, Inkelas, Briggs, and Rhee, 1997) and tend to attend higher-prestige institutions (Hearn, 1991). Socioeconomic status and level of social capital in students' families also relate to academic achievement (Goddard, 2003) and attainment (Conley, 2001; Mullen, 2009). Finally, students' high school context shapes their enrollment decisions. This influence is felt through the types of curricular and college preparation available (Lucas and Good, 2001; Solorzano and Ornelas, 2004; Teranishi, Allen, and Solorzano, 2004), relationships between the school and higher education institutions (Mullen, 2009; Wolniak and Engberg, 2007), the school context's impact on parental involvement (Rowan-Kenyon, Bell, and Perna, 2008), and academic achievement in the school itself (Gardner, Ritblatt, and Beatty, 2000). Counseling resources also affect students' institutional choices (Perna and others, 2008), in terms of both the availability of counselors to assist with college preparation and planning and the types of information provided by counselors. High school resources are affected by the socioeconomic status of the student population (Perna and others, 2008), resulting in inequitable access to information and coursework essential to college preparation for students from different socioeconomic, racial, and ethnic backgrounds.

Hossler and Gallagher's Model in Recent Research

Hossler and Gallagher's three-stage model of college choice (1987) provided a jumping-off point for the research of many scholars over the last twenty years. Some studies tested and expanded on particular phases of the model, while others used the model as a foundation for new models. This section summarizes the research that expands on and critiques Hossler and Gallagher's model, leading to a discussion of the implications of attempting to develop a comprehensive model of college choice.

A number of studies set out to refine and explore the predisposition stage of Hossler and Gallagher's model. For example, Bouse and Hossler (1991) explored factors "associated with student predisposition" (p. 12) and found that parents' education, parental encouragement, and conversations about college with students were related to predisposition for white male and female students and for black females. For black males, only parental encouragement was related to a predisposition to attend college. For all students, grade point average was positively related to predisposition. These findings were echoed in a 1992 study by Hossler and Stage, who found that parent education and socioeconomic status were important factors in predisposition but that parental expectations for college attendance were the most significant. Lillard and Gerner (1999) also built on the concept of predisposition, finding that family composition had an impact on students' postsecondary plans. Noting that students from disrupted families were less likely to attend college and particularly less likely to attend selective colleges, the authors posited that a number of factors related to family disruptions lead to these choices. Exploring factors such as peers' academic aspirations, lower school performance, lower participation in extracurricular activities, and reduced family income, the authors argued that although "it is plausible to argue that family disruption causes the above negative consequences, it must also be observed that one is more likely to observe disruption among families" that are characterized by these factors (p. 721). The studies reported here expand our understanding of how predisposition develops.

Hossler and Vesper (1993) examined the complex process of aspiration formation through the lens of college savings. They found that parents' understanding of the postsecondary environment related to their college savings behaviors, which affected the educational aspirations of both parents and children. Although these findings related to the formation of aspirations, which is part of the predisposition stage, they also have implications for the search phase in that parents' savings behaviors are related to the information they have about postsecondary education (Ikenberry and Hartle, 1998). Related to the issue of planning, Bers and Galowich (2002) used Hossler and Gallagher's model to study the college choice processes of community college students. They found that students who planned earlier for college were less likely to attend community colleges. For these students, factors related to socioeconomic status and students' uncertainties about college were more important to college choice than institutional reputation or the influence of friends and family members. These findings illustrate that the college choice process is not as linear as it appears. This complexity as well as questions about predisposition for students from populations traditionally underrepresented in higher education led researchers such as Hurtado, Inkelas, Briggs, and Rhee (1997) to call for a renewed effort to improve our understanding of the factors that lead to predisposition. Given the intersections of factors that play into the formation of individuals' predisposition, further exploration of predisposition is an area ripe for increased qualitative research. Well-designed qualitative studies have the potential to dig deeply into the individual processes of aspiration formation and explore patterns across and within various groups.

Although the process of institutional selection appears to be less complex than the formation of predisposition, a number of factors play into this stage of Hossler and Gallagher's model as well, and several studies attempted to clarify their impact. In their study, Galotti and Mark (1994) examined the decision-making process of 322 college-bound high school students over the course of their senior year. The authors found that the sources of information used by students changed over the course of the year, from active search to interactive search (Hossler, Schmit, and Vesper, 1999), as print materials gave way to college representatives as the primary source of information. Further, differences were apparent in how students used their parents as information sources by parental education, with more highly educated parents not surprisingly consulted more frequently than those with less education.

Related to Galotti and Mark's study (1994) of how students use information, Hossler, Schmit, and Vesper (1999) further explored Hossler and Gallagher's model to examine how the influence of college choice factors varied as students progressed through the model's three phases. In the predisposition phase, parental encouragement, level of parents' education, student achievement, high school involvement, and peers were influential. In the search phase, students began to use external sources of information about college. When students entered the choice phase, the authors found that most stayed within the choice set established through the influence of internal factors but that institutional choice was largely based on external information sources. Martin and Dixon's research (1991) examined the role of locus of control on the choice process and found that students whose locus of control is outside themselves are more influenced by others than those with an internal locus of control. Interestingly, externals from higher-income families were more open to outside influences than those from lower-income families.

Clarify.

Also related to the concept of institutional choice is Nora's study (2004) exploring how psychosocial elements, which Nora termed "the heart of the process" (p. 197), shape students' institutional choices. Nora found that students relied more on these psychosocial elements (sense of personal acceptance at the institution, family encouragement, a match between their academic interests and institutional offerings [p. 194]) than on choice factors described in earlier literature (grades, institutional characteristics, high school experiences, and preparation). Psychosocial factors were significant for students attending institutions representing various levels of selectivity and for white students and students of color. Nora argued that recognizing and acting on the psychosocial elements of institutional choice can also lead to greater persistence in college. Nora's work adds a layer of complexity to the institutional choice process and draws attention to the nuances that drive students' decisions.

Further exploring the complexity of the institutional choice process, DesJardins, Ahlburg, and McCall (2006) developed a model of college application, admission, enrollment, and financial aid. Studying a population of Iowa students who sent test scores to a university, the authors examined who actually applied for admission, those who were admitted and rejected, and how financial aid affected their decisions to enroll. These authors found that students' *expectation* of aid shaped their enrollment decisions. This finding built on previous studies that examined the influence of financial aid (Curs and Singell, 2002; Dynarski, 2003; Van der Klaaw, 2002), leading the authors to urge institutions not to disappoint students whose expectations of aid influence their application to and enrollment in specific institutions. All the studies described above can help high schools and higher education institutions tailor the structure and distribution of postsecondary information to students and parents by targeting certain types of information to students at particular phases in the process.

Critiques of Hossler and Gallagher's Model

The preceding paragraphs outlined studies that sought to build on the understanding of college choice presented in Hossler and Gallagher's model. Another body of research has questioned the applicability of the model for populations of students traditionally underrepresented in higher education, specifically students of color and students from low socioeconomic backgrounds. This literature represents a shift in focus to one of access and equity for the increasingly diverse student population in the United States today, drawing attention to the stratification in higher education and the need to better understand factors at its root. This literature is further synthesized in the next two chapters.

Perna and Titus (2004) examined how state policies affect students' college choice processes. The authors determined that state policies such as higher education appropriations, tuition policies, financial aid, and elementary and secondary education were related to the choice process. The authors also found that students from lower socioeconomic backgrounds were less likely to enroll in college and, in particular, four-year institutions. This finding echoes those of others who examined the role of social class in college choice (Hossler, Schmit, and Vesper, 1999; McDonough, 1997; Teranishi and others, 2004) and argued that social class shapes college choice processes.

Some research frames the issue of low college attendance by lower socioeconomic status students as going beyond student background characteristics to broader sociological phenomena. For example, using the work of Pierre Bourdieu (1977) to frame their work, McDonough, Ventresca, and Outcalt (2000) used field analysis to examine how the structure of college choice has changed. The authors argued that as sources of information have moved from high schools and higher education institutions to the private sector, with an emphasis on technology as an information source, the college choice field is becoming privatized. Low-income students do not have the same access to privatized technology-based sources of information as wealthier students. Similarly, McDonough, Antonio, Walpole, and Perez (1998) found that the structure of college rankings benefits higher socioeconomic and academically achieving students who have "college knowledge" (p. 530) in their families and who use private college guidance counselors.

These students, the authors found, rely on rankings to determine their institutional choice far more than students from lower socioeconomic backgrounds and first-generation college students. Both of these articles point out that although many see the use of technology and rankings as increasing access to information, these sources of information more readily appeal to and are disproportionately used by upper-income students. These findings illustrate that models such as Hossler and Gallagher's, which assume that all students have equal access to information about postsecondary education, fall short of explaining the college choice process of students who are not able to tap into some information sources.

Kern (2000) and Cabrera and LaNasa (2001) questioned how well Hossler and Gallagher's model fits students they call "disadvantaged" (p. 119). Kern's study focused on urban high school students of color whose families did not have a tradition of college attendance. She found that parental encouragement was the most significant factor influencing students' college aspirations and noted that, combined with active and supportive counseling from high school personnel, parents could exert a tremendous impact on students' postsecondary plans. At the same time, many students in her study indicated that financial issues were a barrier to their college enrollment. Similarly, Cabrera and LaNasa compared low and high socioeconomic status students on their ability to complete three essential tasks for college attendance: minimal academic qualification, high school graduation, and completion of admissions applications. These authors found significant differences between the groups of students based on socioeconomic status but also observed that additional factors influenced students' ability to complete the three tasks listed above. These individual-, family-, and school-based practices (pp. 141–142) focus on improving school resources and providing interventions that will aid in academic preparation, increasing information available to parents, which contributes to higher levels of parent involvement, and assisting students and parents with curriculum and financial planning, starting as early as the eighth grade. Both of these studies emphasized that a model of college choice must include attention to the specific choice processes for students of color and "disadvantaged" (p. 119) students. Intensive qualitative studies would contribute to developing this body of research by exploring in depth the individual choice processes of students from populations underrepresented in higher education and further illuminating systemic inequities that shape their choice processes and decisions.

Financial concerns repeatedly appear in the literature as playing a part in students' postsecondary choices (Callendar and Jackson, 2008; Heller, 1997, 1999; Hossler, 2000; Kim, 2004; Paulsen and St. John, 2002; Reay, Davies, David, and Ball, 2001). Paulsen and St. John (2002) expanded on Hossler and Gallagher's model by focusing on a "financial nexus model" (p.193) that spans college choice to persistence. In essence, the authors sought to understand how financial issues played into both college choice and the decision to stay in college for students from different socioeconomic backgrounds. The authors found that social class shapes postsecondary education choices in two ways: "directly in response to prices and subsidies, and indirectly through perceptions and expectations of affordability of college costs" (p. 228). Paulsen and St. John's model added to existing research on the choice process with its attention to the increasingly diverse population of students approaching college age, which warrants the study of specific groups, and the contexts within which these groups of students make college-related decisions (p. 192). Questions about the fit of a model for diverse groups of students led other researchers to modify or expand on Hossler and Gallagher's model or to develop new models explaining the process by which students make postsecondary education decisions.

Emerging College Choice Models

Although many researchers focused on testing and critiquing Hossler and Gallagher's model, others set out to develop new models that more accurately described the choice processes of a wide range of students, often building on the foundations laid by Hossler and Gallagher. For example, Cabrera and LaNasa's model of college choice (2000) reflects Hossler and Gallagher's model in its recognition that students go through various stages as they consider postsecondary options. These authors conceptualize the choice process as including direct and indirect influences on the ultimate decision. For instance, the availability of information about higher education influences a student's aspirations, which directly affect his or her choice, but information also affects parental encouragement and the "saliency" (p. 7) of a student's choices. Likewise, parental characteristics such as education, employment, and income influence a student's academic ability, early aspirations, qualifications for college, and parental involvement. One strength of Cabrera and LaNasa's model, which was developed through a review of literature, is that it illustrates the domino effect of certain factors in the process, illuminating the complexity masked by the linear structure of Hossler and Gallagher's model.

Perna's conceptual model of college choice (2006), which also illustrates the complexity of the process, moves away from Hossler and Gallagher's approach. Perna's model includes four layers of influence on students' college choice. The first, individual habitus, borrows from Bourdieu's work (1977) and includes an understanding of the student's background characteristics. Factors such as race, ethnicity, social class, parents' education, and the presence of social and cultural capital all combine to form an individual's habitus, from which postsecondary aspirations and plans arise. Habitus acts as an unconscious lens through which individuals view their options and make decisions based on what feels comfortable for them, given their background characteristics (Bergerson, 2007). The next layer of Perna's model is the school and community context. Perna noted that individual decisions must be viewed in light of this context, which includes school characteristics such as availability of counseling, size, and the overall knowledge of college in the school and communities that share ideas about education that influence students' aspirations and plans. The higher education context is the next layer of Perna's model, which assumes that factors such as nearby institutions, regional cultures and norms, and the region's "tradition and philosophy towards both higher and K–12 education" (p. 143) affect the context within which students decide about college enrollment. Finally, Perna attended to the social, economic, and policy context, which includes labor market trends, population demographics, and policies that support or discourage college enrollment. Recognizing that the context in which a student makes college enrollment decisions shapes this process, Perna's model accounts for individual differences as well as how various contexts shape decisions and has the potential to shape the future of college choice research. Given its relatively recent arrival in the field, however, not much effort has been made to test and refine the model.

Similar to Perna's contextual model is Tierney and Venegas's cultural framework model (2009), which posits that educational, familial, community, and out-of-class environments all play into students' choices. These authors reject the linear thinking behind rational choice models (presented below) and instead frame students as decision makers who weigh influences from all four environments as they make choices. Writing specifically about the process of making college choice decisions in light of financial aid availability, the authors contended that the cultural framework allows researchers to better understand how different environments have varying levels of influence over students' choices. For example, rather than seeing all high schools as singular entities that provide the same information to all students, the cultural framework allows for the fact that different schools provide different resources to students and that even within schools, students from underrepresented populations receive different information from white middle- and upper-class students. Tierney and Venegas's model is promising for researchers and professionals who view the college choice process through an access and equity lens, but because it is a newcomer to the field, its nuances are as yet unexplored.

Another model emphasizes the complexity of the college choice process but in a different way. Henrickson's model of college choice (2002) uses agent-based modeling to focus on the interactions between students and institutions during the choice process. Henrickson's model considered two types of agents: students and higher education institutions. Each has a microlevel, individual decision to make; students choose whether to enroll, and institutions choose whether to admit students. By observing the interactions between these agents, researchers can determine the "macro-scale consequence" (p. 407) of enrollment patterns in higher education. Henrickson suggested that this model could lead to more detailed understandings of the choice process by focusing on the peer group's influence and the multiple process steps in a single study. Henrickson's model, however, does not account for individual- or social identity group–based influences on the college choice process and, as such, needs refinement to significantly contribute to furthering our understanding of the college choice process.

Although Perna's and Henrickson's models moved away from individual student choice processes, Morgan (2002) honed in on the processes through which individuals develop commitment to their educational aspirations and found that here, too, students interact with their context as they decide where to enroll. Morgan's model builds on the rational choice model by looking at "the social processes that generate the costs, benefits, and preferences on which individuals rely when making expected utility calculations" (p. 388). To do so, Morgan modeled how students develop their beliefs about the future and commit to actions that move them toward those beliefs. Morgan explored the impact of three dimensions of prefigurative commitment to future beliefs: purposive, normative, and imitative. Most important is purposive commitment, in which students determine whether to go to college based on whether it is in their best interest. Purposive commitment is influenced by information. Complete information leads to development of high levels of commitment to the future; incomplete information results in goal ambivalence and fewer behaviors leading to goal attainment. Normative commitment, based on the influence of significant others in one's life, and imitative commitment, based on the decisions of similar others, are second-order dimensions that influence the development of purposive commitment. One strength of Morgan's model is its recognition that rational choices are made in contextual constraints such as normative and imitative forces, thus expanding on rational choice theory, which dominates the economic approach to college enrollment. The model also draws in the sociological approach by providing ways to operationalize variables thought to influence choice such as social and cultural capital and habitus (Bourdieu, 1977). Other researchers drew more exclusively on rational choice theory in their models.

Breen and Goldthorpe (1997) and Pitre (2006b) both build on rational choice as an element of the college decision-making process. Breen and Goldthorpe set out to explain the continued class stratification in the U.S. higher education environment. Rather than focusing solely on economic returns on an investment in education, these authors posited that students consider three factors: the cost of education, the likelihood of their success in higher education, and the belief that they will actualize their expected outcomes. Decisions in this model are based on risk aversion. Upper- and middle-class students make decisions that they perceive reduce the risk of falling to a lower social class. For students from lower social classes, the chances of succeeding in higher education and accessing the desired outcomes are lower than for students in higher social classes, so their risk aversion is driven by a desire to avoid spending limited resources on an action that they believe has little chance of generating the desired return. Based on their findings, Breen and Goldthorpe argued that although rational processes are more nuanced than they often appear, they still form the core of "patterns of educational choices in [the] aggregate" (p. 299).

Like Breen and Goldthorpe (1997), Pitre (2006b) used the rational choice model to understand stratification in higher education. Pitre's focus was on the college-going behaviors of primarily African American students, which he used to develop a model of reasoned action. In this model, behavioral intentions interact with attitude and subjective norms and lead to enrollment decisions. The model begins by examining how individual beliefs about education and the evaluation of the possible outcomes of educational attainment interact to form attitudes and expectations about college. At the same time, normative beliefs, influenced by contextual factors, interact with motivations to comply with norms to produce the student's sense of the "opinions of significant others with regard to college attendance" (p. 39). The student's attitude toward college and subjective norms interact to form what Pitre calls the "predisposition intention" (p. 39), which leads to behaviors such as applying for college. Although appealing because of its straightforward attention to an individual's ability to collect information and make rational decisions based on that information, rational choice theories may oversimplify a complex process that is clearly influenced by context as much as objective information (Tierney and Venegas, 2009). Further, given the fact that students of color and lower socioeconomic status students have less access to information, choice models based on rational choice theory fall short of accounting for these differences.

Although new theoretical approaches to college choice are in the process of being developed, it is clear that the complexity of environments, systemic issues, and individual differences complicate the process for individual students and constrain the degree to which a comprehensive model can explain this process. Rather than focus on the development of new models, some researchers have looked outside the college choice literature for lenses that can shed new light on their examination of the ways students decide whether and where to go to college. The following section turns to these lenses.

Alternative Lenses for Viewing the College Choice Process

College choice literature includes a number of studies that use social reproduction and cultural wealth (Garcia and Guerra, 2004) lenses to view the intricacies of the college choice process and to reveal the systemic inequities that complicate the process for students of color and lower-socioeconomic students. Bourdieu's social reproduction theory (1977, 1987, 1993) posits that individuals operating in social institutions such as schools make socially constrained choices that serve to reproduce the existing social order. Individuals with the kinds of capital that are recognized and rewarded by social organizations are able to navigate those systems more easily than those whose capital is not valued. Building on the notion of capital, the cultural wealth lens encourages social institutions and the actors in them to recognize the capital that students from nondominant cultures bring with them to social settings. This capital includes familial support, language, and an emphasis on community building. The cultural wealth lens argues that when students' cultural capital is recognized and valued by schools, they achieve higher levels of success.

Bourdieu: Social Reproduction Theory

Three concepts provide a foundation for social reproduction theory: habitus, capital, and field (Bourdieu, 1977). Bourdieu conceived of habitus as "a system of dispositions [that] acts as a mediation between structures and practice" (p. 487). In a particular field, members use habitus to determine their available choices; habitus delineates their actions. The largely subconscious limiting of available options that occurs in a person's habitus acts to reproduce the existing social order, as individuals often do not see choices outside what they perceive to be available to their particular social group. Reay (2004) pointed out that habitus is a state of mind (p. 441) that influences behavior even when individuals move out of the context in which their habitus developed. Bourdieu (Bourdieu and Wacquant, 1992) noted that habitus produces specific actions only in particular fields and that the fit between field and habitus produces actions that "yield a variety of outcomes ranging from perfect mutual fit . . . to radical disjunction" (p. 130). Used in the college choice arena, habitus is the context in which students consider their postsecondary education options, from whether to go to college to where.

The second key concept is capital (Bourdieu, 1977). Capital is a form of power in a given field. Three types of capital exist: economic, social, and cultural. Economic capital describes resources that have monetary value. Economic capital shapes students' college choices, as seen in the number of studies in which financial issues affect students' decisions about whether and where to go to college. Families with higher amounts of economic capital are less constrained when making institutional choices than families whose economic capital is limited.

Social capital is seen as an individual's valuable networks or connections. Social capital interacts with economic capital in the process of accumulating cultural capital. According to Bourdieu (1993), economic capital "provides the conditions for freedom from economic necessity" (p. 68), which, when accompanied by social capital, allow individuals the time and connections necessary to invest in the accumulation of cultural capital. Independent from economic capital, social capital affects what students know about available educational choices and where they get that information (McDonough, 1997). In a wealthy college-educated family, potential students are exposed to information about postsecondary education options. They, their families, and their peers speak the language of higher education, understand how admissions processes work, and are aware of scholarships and financial aid options. Lower socioeconomic status families do not have these types of networks, which may result in limited access to information and resources about higher education options.

Cultural capital represents an individual's cultural status and knowledge, including "verbal facility, general cultural awareness, aesthetic preferences, information about the school system, and educational credentials" (Swartz, 1997, p. 75). Cultural capital legitimates an individual's power. Cultural capital held by a student's family also plays a role in how much and where he or she collects information about educational opportunities. Bourdieu (1977) also noted that the value of a degree "depends on the economic and social values of the person who possesses it, in as much as the yield of social capital . . . depends upon the economic and social capital [that] can be put to its valorization" (p. 506). Although education allows any individual to convert economic capital into cultural capital, the degree to which it occurs is determined by the amount of capital that person took into the field in the first place. In higher education, a student who has extensive social capital and uses her connections to secure a prestigious position after college may find that her degree is more valuable than that of a student who does not have the same connections (Bergerson, 2007).

The third notion presented by Bourdieu is field (1993). Capital has value only in a particular field. Each field is distinct, with its own rules. Bourdieu argued that in a given field, individuals compete for the available capital, or power, with the goal of safeguarding their positions in that field. Ultimately, those whose capital is legitimized in the field define the rules of the game. Bourdieu and Wacquant (1992) argued that the strategies or "practice" people use to compete in a field are "suggested" (p. 128) by their habitus and available capital. In Bourdieu's approach, practice is the act of living life and functioning in different fields. Bourdieu and Wacquant noted that "practice is the product of a particular economic condition, defined by the possession of the minimum economic and cultural capital necessary actually to perceive and seize the 'potential opportunities' formally offered to all" (p. 124). Because it is the result of both action and interaction, practice is not a static concept. Rather, it changes as an individual makes decisions based on habitus and capital in different fields. Field in the college choice process is the higher education environment, where students and their families determine their place through the amassing of information that is processed through the lens of their habitus and available capital. As habitus and capital shape behaviors, students may act in ways that are not consistent with comprehensive models and conceptions of how they should behave. Bourdieu's framework then becomes one way of explaining and understanding students' practice.

Taken together, the ideas of habitus, capital, and field provide the foundation for Bourdieu's framework (1977) of social reproduction. In essence, this theory posits that social inequities are reproduced as individuals "practice" in their fields, based on their habitus and access to various types of capital.

Social institutions such as schools, colleges, and universities award students who already have capital that is valued in that field. Students who do not possess valued capital have a more difficult time in these social systems and often choose not to participate in the same ways as their capital-possessing peers. In this way, the existing hierarchies in the system are reproduced, and ultimately, Bourdieu argued, systems that are intended to level societal inequities actually end up contributing to stratification. This focus on systemic inequities and individuals' place in these systems makes Bourdieu's framework especially useful for examining the college choice process. Although college is one way many in the United States believe they can "get ahead," for many students it is not that simple. The continued stratification of higher education is evidence that education's role as "the great equalizer" has not been fulfilled. The cultural wealth paradigm builds on Bourdieu's notions of capital, emphasizing the importance of recognizing and rewarding the variety of capital that individuals bring to social organizations to enhance their navigation of those systems.

A Cultural Wealth Paradigm

For decades, the lower performance of students of color in education has been viewed and explained through a deficit approach. According to Valencia (1997), this approach "posits that students who fail in school do so because of alleged internal deficiencies (such as cognitive and/or motivational limitations) or shortcomings socially linked to the youngster—such as familial deficits or dysfunctions" (p. xi). An example of a deficit explanation for the underrepresentation of students of color in higher education is one that claims that education is not important to communities of color. This explanation holds the victim responsible for his or her own situation, allowing institutional and systemic aspects of the problem to remain unquestioned. Continued use of the deficit approach prohibits the types of change necessary to change social systems and institutions, because the victims of inequities cannot by themselves drive those changes. To implement recommendations for increasing access to higher education for students of color suggested by researchers, practitioners and policymakers must embrace a different paradigm, one that focuses on the assets students of color bring to the process and allows for systemic and institutional barriers to be identified and addressed.

Cultural wealth, or an asset-oriented perspective (Garcia and Guerra, 2004; Villalpando and Solorzano, 2005), is a paradigm that responds to this need. The underlying assumption of this perspective is that families of color do value education and that individuals from different communities bring with them cultural values that have a positive effect on their educational experiences—*if* they are validated by educational systems. Villalpando and Solorzano suggested that these assets can be seen as forms of social and cultural capital that have typically not been valued in educational settings.

Villalpando and Solorzano (2005) noted that the value parents place on education, applied to the college choice process, is a form of capital that benefits students of color in reaching their postsecondary aspirations. Most college choice research, however, focuses on parents' education, which is not a type of capital many students of color possess. Language is another area that affects many students of color in education. Gandara (1999) noted that one positive factor in the successful navigation of the college choice process of the students in her study was literacy, both in Spanish and English. Yet K–12 schooling systems force many students into English as a Second Language programs (Gonzales, Stoner, and Jovel, 2003) that hinder their progress toward postsecondary education. A cultural wealth approach would encourage literacy in multiple languages, recognizing its value in educational and employment settings, and reward the acquisition and maintenance of this skill. Cultural wealth models would argue that bilingual capability is an asset rather than a deficit and that students' second languages should be incorporated into their educational experiences. Moving from deficit to cultural wealth explanations for students' success and failure in education allows for the implementation of policies and practices that have the potential to reshape the experiences of students of color in educational systems, ensuring that policies, practices, and future research address individual, community, institutional, and systemic factors contributing to the lower participation of students of color in higher education.

Chapter Summary

Comprehensive models of college choice opened windows onto the processes students use to decide whether and where to go to college. The most widely cited comprehensive college choice model is Hossler and Gallagher's three-stage model (1987), which has remained the threshold from which many studies of college choice have evolved. As the college-going population grew increasingly diverse, however, it became clear that this model could not adequately explain the nuances of a complex process for students stemming from a wide variety of cultural and socioeconomic backgrounds. This chapter reviewed Hossler and Gallagher's model and the research that expands on and critiques the model's three phases. Much of this research is quantitative in nature and weighs the predictive capacity of numerous variables in determining how and why students will make the postsecondary decisions they do. Well-designed qualitative research is clearly needed that has the ability to fill in the knowledge gaps left by these quantitative studies, particularly related to how students of color and lower socioeconomic students engage in the process of deciding whether and where to go to college.

Additionally, the last ten years have seen the emergence of new models that illuminate the ways context shapes the choice processes of individual students. Whether based on layers of context (Perna, 2006; Tierney and Venegas, 2009) or focused on the complex interactions between individuals and institutions (Henrickson, 2002), these models move away from assuming that all students have equitable access to information and resources necessary for engaging in a college choice process, which is a shortcoming of earlier models. In addition to attempting to develop new models to explain the college choice process, researchers are employing different paradigms, allowing them to illustrate the societal and systemic inequities that shape students' postsecondary decisions. Taken as a whole, this recent research exemplifies the trend outlined in the previous chapter toward an understanding of college choice that aims to resolve the continued stratification of higher education in the United States.

College Choice for Lower Socioeconomic Students

R ESEARCH DELVING INTO HOW COLLEGE PREDISPOSITION is formed would better serve diverse student populations as they embark on the college choice process (Hurtado, Inkelas, Briggs, and Rhee, 1997). A number of researchers have responded to this call by exploring the roles of family socioeconomic status and social and cultural capital in the college choice process. This research explores how background characteristics affect students' access to information about higher education and educational aspirations and expectations for college predisposition. This chapter introduces the numerous studies that use Bourdieu's concepts (1977, 1987, 1993) to frame a better understanding of the college choice processes of lower socioeconomic students. Although the college choice experiences of students from lower socioeconomic backgrounds are in many ways similar to those of students from higher-resource backgrounds, the literature presented in this chapter illuminates the nuances that differentiate the experiences of students engaging in decisions of whether and where to go to college. In sum, the research reflects the trend of college choice research toward examining issues of access and equity for lower socioeconomic students.

Issues of Access for Lower Socioeconomic Students

College choice is a complex construct that incorporates students' college aspirations, their expectations of those aspirations becoming a reality, the beginning of their plans, and the steps taken to actualize those aspirations. Family background, parental encouragement, the context in which students grow up, academic ability, schooling experiences, family structure, and information about postsecondary options all contribute to this process. Many students begin planning for college as early as the eighth grade (Cabrera and LaNasa, 2001). In one study exploring the college choice process of women, several women stated that, in their families, not going to college was not an option (Bergerson, Heiselt, Aiken-Wisniewski, and Thompson, 2005). At the same time, other youth never even consider college as an option. This dichotomy has led a number of researchers to explore, define, and attempt to explain how background characteristics, social context, and school experiences interconnect to form students' predispositions about higher education. Significant attention has been paid to college choice generally, but much remains to learn about how students who come from lower socioeconomic backgrounds experience the process.

Family background characteristics are thought to be a major factor in college enrollment decisions. Parents' education and income are frequently included as elements of family background characteristics that affect educational aspirations (Bouse and Hossler, 1991; Conley, 2001; Hossler and Stage, 1992; Reynolds and Pemberton, 2001). Several studies found that family structure also plays a role. For example, Lillard and Gerner (1999) found that students from disrupted families were less likely to aspire to a college education, and Mare (1997) found that when parents had higher levels of education, the impact of fertility on students' educational aspirations was mitigated. In families with lower levels of intergenerational mobility, as indicated by levels of education from one generation to the next, larger families resulted in lower educational aspirations. Family structures such as size and disruption affect parents' aspirations for their children's education, which affects expectations, as parents and children realize what is realistic for their families.

Another factor in college choice is parental expectations. Hossler and Stage (1992) found that parents' educational expectations had the greatest influence on students' college predisposition. Related to parental expectations is parental encouragement, which includes both emotional support and behavioral components such as saving for children's higher education (Hossler and Vesper, 1993). Kern's study of urban high school students (2000) illustrated the importance of parental encouragement; more than 75 percent of her study participants indicated that this encouragement was vital to their college aspirations. Yet parents who themselves do not have a college education may be constrained in their efforts to adequately support and encourage their children to achieve their educational expectations. Many lower socioeconomic parents hope that their children will receive this guidance and support in their school settings, but the research presented below suggests that it is not always the case.

School context contributes to postsecondary choices. For example, Goddard (2003) found that in schools with high-trust relationships among parents, students, and teachers, students achieve academically, encouraging a predisposition toward college. Perna and others (2008) found that state and district factors affect the culture around and resources for college counseling in high schools. High-resource schools typically have more resources for and a culture more supportive of college guidance counseling, which means students in low-resource schools who need assistance and information the most have limited access to them. Student academic achievement also contributes to whether and where students go to college. In Hossler and Stage's study (1992), grades had a significant relationship to postsecondary education aspirations, a finding supported by Nora's study (2004).

Finally, it is clear that information shapes the college choice process (Grodsky and Jones, 2007; Ikenberry and Hartle, 1998). The assumption is that access to a range of reliable information encourages students to consider postsecondary education as an option. Access to information is affected by social networks and neighborhood context (Grodsky and Jones, 2007) and plays a role in motivating parental behaviors that demonstrate encouragement of college attendance (Hossler and Vesper, 1993), including saving for college and actively assisting children with completing admission and financial aid applications (Hossler, Schmit, and Vesper, 1999). Students and families from lower socioeconomic backgrounds experience constraints on their access to information. For example, lower-resource schools do not have the means to support parents' and students' need for accurate postsecondary information. Limited access to this information results in limited access to postsecondary opportunities.

Although knowing what factors play into college choice is important, it is still unclear how these factors specifically shape the process for lower socioeconomic students. One theoretical lens used extensively to shed light on this issue is that of social reproduction theory (Bourdieu, 1977). Specifically, the concepts of social and cultural capital, habitus, and field (Bourdieu, 1993) have been applied conceptually and empirically to explore the college choice process. The next section describes how Bourdieu's concepts shape the discussion of college choice for lower socioeconomic students.

Linking Bourdieu to College Choice

Several researchers used Bourdieu's ideas to develop deeper understandings of the college choice process. The analysis of these studies is organized parallel to the factors contributing to the postsecondary decision process described above, beginning with parents' education and income, parental expectations, and parental encouragement. School context and academic achievement are then viewed through Bourdieu's lenses. Next the section looks at the literature examining access to information. Several studies also incorporate Bourdieu's ideas to examine the concept of "fit," both as an institutional factor and as an element of deciding whether to attend college at all. Finally, the section introduces several authors who used Bourdieu's concepts to frame their critical stance regarding the applicability of traditional models of college choice to lower socioeconomic students' experiences, emphasizing the role of these ideas in moving the field of college choice to addressing issues of access through recommendations for practice, policy, and research.

Parental Education and Income

Both parental income and education play into the college choice processes of low socioeconomic students. Parental education and income are confounded variables (Conley, 2001), meaning that parents with less education typically have lower incomes. The result is that for students from low socioeconomic backgrounds, cost is a significant factor in the college choice process. Lower socioeconomic students whose parents do not have the knowledge or resources to demonstrate these forms of support may find that their postsecondary options are limited. This situation leads to greater sensitivity to cost and financial aid availability in the search and choice stages of the process.

Cost sensitivity is greater for students from lower socioeconomic backgrounds (Paulsen and St. John, 2002; St. John and Asker, 2001) than for upper- and middle-class students. Keane (2002) also found that the effect of tuition changes was greater for low socioeconomic students. The stories of the low-income students in Bloom's study (2007) reiterated this fact; students repeatedly talked about their inability to finance what their middle- and upper-income peers felt were reasonable amounts for college. Some research found that low-income families resist taking on loan debt to finance college (Bloom, 2007; Callendar and Jackson, 2008). Keane (2002) and Gladieux (2004) supported this argument, noting that working-class students are more likely to be employed during college to mitigate the need to borrow. Reay, Davies, David, and Ball (2001) illustrated how the need to work limited students' enrollment options. Both Keane (2002) and Ellwood and Kane (2000) argued that parents' contribution to students' college education makes a difference in where students go to college. Their studies found that the influence of parents' contribution is greater than the debt aversion for low socioeconomic students. This finding led Keane to argue that tuition subsidies were the most effective way to alleviate class stratification in higher education. Keane's argument is reiterated by Gladieux (2004), whose report on the affordability of higher education for low socioeconomic students called for "a restoration of need-based principles for financing students in higher education, in the interest of equity as well as efficient allocation of public and private resources" (p. 17), a recommendation echoed by Perna, Steele, Woda, and Hibbert (2005). These studies show a link between the enrollment decisions of low socioeconomic students, institutional cost, and the availability of financial aid. In Bourdieu's terms, the lack of economic capital constrains these students' ability to generate social and cultural capital through college attendance.

Cabrera and LaNasa (2001) found that parental education played a "pivotal" (p. 134) role in students' ability to gain the qualifications necessary for enrollment in higher education, including graduating from high school. Parental education and family income were two measures of social origin in Lopez-Turley, Santos, and Ceja's study (2007) of college expectations across cohorts of students from 1972 to 1992. Over that period, the impact of income on higher education expectations was stable, but the effect of parents' education level increased significantly. Lopez-Turley, Santos, and Ceja also found that only the students with the most advantages in terms of parental education and income were likely to apply to highly selective institutions. These authors tie educational opportunity expectations to Bourdieu's concept of habitus (1977), noting that educational expectations are based partly on "unconscious assessments of what is realistic" (p. 1202).

Karen (2002) supported the finding that family income and parents' education play a role in college choice, noting in particular that the father's education level influenced students' college enrollment. Although both Cabrera and LaNasa (2001) and Lopez-Turley, Santos, and Ceja (2007) used Bourdieu's concepts to help explain stratification in higher education, Karen took it a step further, arguing that upper-class families contribute to social stratification in their effort to retain their dominant role in society. This concept echoes Bourdieu's argument (1993) that individuals compete for available capital in an effort to amass enough to secure their place in the social system. Karen posited that recent court cases challenging affirmative action, statutes such as California's Proposition 209, and the trend toward merit-based financial aid provide evidence of an intentional focus on elite students in higher education. Although Karen's argument makes sense from Bourdieu's perspective, no empirical evidence supports it. How conscious individuals are of their desire to maintain their social status is still in question.

Related to the effect of parents' income on predisposition is Hofferth, Boisjoly, and Duncan's study of access to time or money resources (1998). These researchers found that time and money from outside the immediate family had a positive impact on the college enrollment of higher-income youth but had no effect on lower-income students. The authors deduced that although social capital (defined as access to outside resources) does not substitute for income, it facilitates the use of that income. Parents' networks were important to the college enrollment of upper-income students, indicating that access to capital is a factor in educational attainment. McGrath, Swisher, Elder, and Conger (2001) found a similar trend among rural students. The parents of students in their study who moved out of the agricultural milieu and into college had extensive community and school networks, similar to parents who themselves had participated in higher education, indicating the importance of social capital in educational attainment.

It is clear from these studies that parents do shape their children's educational choices, both in what they do and in who they are. Families with access to lower amounts of capital are also constrained when it comes to high school experiences, disposable income, and access to information. Because of their differential access to these resources, students from lower socioeconomic backgrounds cannot engage in the college choice process in the same ways as their middle- and upper-income peers. Understanding this concept moves the conversation about postsecondary education away from one focused simply on choice to one that struggles with questions of access, which reflects the movement of the field in general.

Educational Expectations and Parental Encouragement

The general college choice literature found that parents' educational expectations and encouragement of students to respond to those expectations shape students' enrollment choices. Although this finding is true for low socioeconomic students and their families, the process is complicated by parents' own educational backgrounds as well as their current socioeconomic status. For instance, Perna's study of white, African American, and Hispanic students' college attendance decisions (2000) found differences in the impact of educational expectations. African Americans' educational expectations are less significant in predicting college attendance than whites and Hispanics. Perna surmised that this situation was a result of lower access to higher education information related to lower social and cultural capital, and called for additional research exploring the contribution of capital to predisposition. Perna's work redirects the conversation from one of choice to one of access.

Cabrera and LaNasa (2001) found in their study of at-risk students that parents' involvement in their children's education was the most notable aspect of parental encouragement for those at the lowest end of the socioeconomic spectrum. Gonzales, Stover, and Jovel (2003) found that Latina and Latino parents' support of their female children's educational aspirations was important, but because many of these parents could provide only emotional support, they were described as having low-volume social capital. Parents' educational backgrounds limited the capital they had to share with their children related to information about or the process of applying to higher education institutions. Tierney (2002) reiterated the importance of both parental support at home and parental involvement in students' learning in the choice process, pointing out that the influence of parents was second only to academic preparation in encouraging students to go to college. Tierney linked this parent role to Bourdieu (1977), pointing out that families are children's primary source of cultural capital.

Family cultural capital also shaped college attendance of students in Kaufman and Gabler's study (2004). These authors found that when students and parents attended museums, students were more likely to attend selective institutions. Parents' museum going alone had an even more significant impact on institutional selectivity. McDonough, Antonio, and Horvat's study (1996) of elite college students also found that museum attendance was an important factor in the formation of students' educational aspirations. Both of these studies are reminiscent of Bourdieu's work (1977), in which he noted the types of cultural capital that signify elite classes, including museum attendance. The findings of Kaufman and Gabler (2004) and McDonough, Antonio, and Horvat (1996) that cultural capital affects college enrollment and in particular enrollment at selective institutions parallels Bourdieu's arguments and contributes to an explanation for the stratification of selective colleges and universities.

Parents encourage their students to reach the family's educational expectations in different ways. Whether engaging in the learning of their children, visiting museums, having a college education themselves, or saving money for college, studies show that both parental actions and characteristics shape aspirations and expectations, which then affect postsecondary enrollment decisions. Bourdieu's concepts help illuminate the inequities in access that some families experience regarding the behaviors and characteristics that increase their children's chances of going to college. Capital, whether economic, social, or cultural, shapes postsecondary opportunities, making the discussion less one of choice and more one of differential access to the information and resources necessary to attain educational aspirations. Parents and families are not the only players in this process, however. Schools also shape opportunity.

School Context and Academic Achievement

Bourdieu (1977) argued that educational institutions contribute to the reproduction of social inequities. This process can be seen in both the ways schools
reward certain types of capital as well as how access to resources shapes the
academic opportunities available to students. Both school context and academic achievement affect students' postsecondary choices. For example, Lareau
(1987) used Bourdieu's concept of cultural capital to explore the relationship
between social class and family–school relationships. Significant to Lareau's
findings was the notion that although the value placed on education by families from different social classes was not different, the "ways in which they
promoted educational success" (p. 81) were. Lareau noted that families with
more capital had more resources to commit to the educational success of their
children, which included access to information about educational options.

Lareau's work (2000) illuminated differences in the schooling experiences of
students who came from low socioeconomic backgrounds. Schools also affect
students' access to information (Horn, 1997). For example, Perna and Titus
(2005) found that students of color tended to attend schools with lower amounts
of capital, often as a result of living in lower-resource neighborhoods. Differences in school resources were significantly related to students' enrollment in
higher education, with students from lower-resource schools more likely to enroll
in two-year than four-year schools. The authors concluded that their findings
"suggest that lower observed college enrollment rates for African Americans and
Hispanics are due in part to lower levels of resources that are available through
the social networks at the schools they attend" (p. 509). McDonough (1998)
also used Bourdieu's notions of organizational capital and culture to examine
how students' high school environments affect the college choices process.
McDonough found that schools and school counselors respond to the expectations of parents regarding college attendance. The school culture is then shaped
by these expectations, which, McDonough argued, are embedded in the habitus
of parents and other school community members. These findings support the
notion that schools as well as individuals have varying levels of capital and that
students with lower amounts of capital tend to attend lower-capital schools.
Clearly this finding has implications for postsecondary enrollment decisions,
with students from lower-resource schools less likely to attend college.

Perna's study (2000) focused specifically on the role of academic preparation, attempting to unpack the relationship between access to capital and academic preparation. Perna found that for African American and Hispanic students, social and cultural capital had as much impact on the likelihood of attending a four-year institution as academic achievement. For whites, academic achievement was a greater predictor of enrollment in a four-year school than social and cultural capital. The role of capital in the enrollment of students of color in Perna's study is of particular interest, given that she also found that African American and Hispanic students on the whole had less access to capital than white students. As a result, students of color with academic achievement that is equal to that of their white peers have less chance of enrolling in four-year higher education institutions than their white peers. This finding led Perna to suggest that researchers continue to explore the impact of social and cultural capital on academic achievement.

Gonzales, Stoner, and Jovel (2003) responded to Perna's call for a deeper understanding of how social and cultural capital shapes the college choice process. These authors developed the concept of "institutional neglect and abuse" to describe actions on the parts of institutional agents that "discourage or produce barriers for college attendance in Latinas" (p. 153). Gonzales and his colleagues argued that Latina students were exposed to high levels of capital or institutional abuse and neglect during high school, and that, depending on which type of exposure prevailed, their college enrollment was either positively or negatively affected. Students in their study who had access to college counselors, considered holders of high-volume social capital, tended to apply to more selective postsecondary institutions, while students at community colleges reported having little to no access to high school counselors. Finally, these researchers found that school context and support were more important in the development of students' educational aspirations than academic ability. Along similar lines, McDonough, Antonio, and Horvat (1996) found that students attending elite colleges and universities formed informal connections with high school teachers, demonstrating access to high-volume social capital, which was necessary to attain the personalized recommendations needed for application to highly selective institutions. Both these studies underline the importance of capital in the college choice process, not only in terms of how much capital students and their families possess but also as related to students' access to certain types of capital.

Access to Information

College search and choice incorporate the gathering and processing of information related to postsecondary education. Hossler and Gallagher's model (1987) assumes that all students have access to this information. Several researchers question this assumption, however, noting constraints on the ability of low socioeconomic students and their families to gather adequate information is limited. For example, McDonough, Antonio, Walpole, and Perez (1998) looked at what types of students used college rankings such as in *U.S. News and World Report* in gathering information. The authors found that students from middle- and upper-class backgrounds were more likely to use this source of information. Further, these students were more likely to apply to and enroll in the high-ranking schools on these lists than low socioeconomic students. This study provides additional evidence of how those who possess capital are at a distinct advantage in the college choice process, particularly when it comes to accessing information.

Two of McDonough's studies used a field analysis approach to examine how the field of college choice is changing and how those changes are advantageous for individuals who possess high levels of capital (McDonough, 1994; McDonough, Ventresca, and Outcalt, 2000). Both studies noted that sources of postsecondary education information are growing increasingly privatized. McDonough (1994) noted that "public high schools have effectively divested themselves of college advisement" (p. 433) and that the private college counselor profession is thriving in an age of competitive college admissions. As a result, students whose families have high levels of economic, cultural, and social capital are advantaged because they have the resources and networks necessary to access private information sources. On the other hand, students from lower socioeconomic backgrounds, who may not have financial resources or simply are not aware of the importance of this resource in the choice process, have less access to information needed to make informed decisions. The outcome of this situation, McDonough, Ventresca, and Outcalt (2000) argued, is social class stratification in higher education. Perna echoed this finding, and Gonzales, Stoner, and Jovel (2003) found that access to high-level "agents of social capital" (p. 152) boosted Latinas' educational expectations. These high-level agents were able to provide information about college, access to higher education opportunities, and emotional support, while lower-level agents could provide only one or two of these resources.

The Role of Habitus in Fit

Bourdieu (1977) conceptualized habitus as a set of dispositions based on an individual's social context that subconsciously guide the decisions that individual makes. In fact, habitus contributes to the perception of a person's fit in any social setting, making it natural that it would influence students' perceptions of fit in higher education. McDonough's study (1997) of the college choice process of students from high schools with different resource levels and cultures illustrated how habitus contributes to the development of students' sense of fit in the higher education environment. Family, friends, and background characteristics such as socioeconomic status and ethnicity shape their habitus, which in turn shape their college choices. McDonough argued that prospective students choose to attend college where they think they belong. In McDonough's study the choice to exclude themselves from particular institutions (usually highly competitive, prestigious, and costly ones) contributed to the reproduction of lower socioeconomic students' status in the existing social order. Nora (2004) also focused on fit, framing his findings in Bourdieu's notions of habitus and cultural capital, both of which, he argued, affected how students perceive institutional fit.

Horvat (2001) also used Bourdieu's concepts to explore college choice, noting that Bourdieu's ideas allow researchers to consider how "preferences and dispositions are rooted in the constructs of race and class at both the individual level in the habitus and in the fields of interaction" and how those preferences and dispositions affect "individual action in social settings" (p. 234). Responding to questions about their choice to attend college, Horvat's participants expressed concerns about how their high school experiences and individual backgrounds did and did not produce a fit with the college environment. Additionally, Mullen (2009) found that fit was important to students who elected to attend college at Yale University, noting that this sense of fit was "inculcated" (p. 21) in students from higher-income families, while lower-income families were often "reluctant" (p. 22) for their children to attend Yale, both because of lack of knowledge about the benefits of attending there and because of concerns about fit.

Also focused on elite college students, McDonough, Antonio, and Horvat (1996) found that they displayed a "high-status habitus" that includes "a system of outlooks, experiences, beliefs, and perceptions that shape attitudes and aspirations" (p. 19). These students came from high-resource families, were high academic achievers, and tended to be white and Asian. This high-status habitus was deemed a fit with the elite colleges and universities these students selected. These researchers called for continued emphasis on exploring how habitus and capital influence students' educational aspirations.

Overall, evidence suggests that habitus affects students' sense of whether and where they fit in the higher education environment. Individual and institutional characteristics also affect this sense of fit. Evidence points to a difference in the college choice experiences of low socioeconomic students and illuminates a number of barriers to their participation in postsecondary education. Bourdieu's concepts help bring these barriers to light, and they also provide a means for addressing them. This contribution is explored in the following discussion of how issues of access and equity fit in the Bourdieu's framework.

Using Bourdieu to Address Issues of Access and Equity

An additional angle of social reproduction theory (Bourdieu, 1977) is that, as with other social classifications (race, ethnicity, sexuality, religion), people often make assumptions about individuals from that classification based on stereotypes. Comments from the African American students in Freeman's study (1997) indicated that students believed school personnel acted on stereotypical assumptions of African Americans not being interested in or skilled enough for higher education. Students commented that the actions based on these assumptions went beyond not supplying adequate postsecondary information to include never even discussing higher education options with them. Freeman's participants described these behaviors contributing to their "loss of hope" and their belief that college was "never an option" (p. 546). When students encounter educational systems that do not reflect their personal and cultural values and are faced with the prospect of having those values "stripped away" (p. 546), they are likely to have a lower sense of worth and a diminished interest in pursuing higher education. McDonough, Antonio, and Trent (1997) echoed Freeman in their assertion that African American cultural capital in the K–12 and higher education systems in the United States is inadequately recognized. The importance of religion, financial aid, and geography were aspects of an African American habitus that these authors found missing in traditional college choice models.

Smith (2007) also called for a reformulation of the way we think about college choice to accentuate the focus on access and equity. Her study of students of color led her to argue that the rules for the field of higher education need to change to accommodate students' different habitus. A teacher complained to Smith that many of his students seemed to take the easy road when considering college options, focusing more on attaining a degree than the status of that degree based on institutional reputation. But for the students, who were largely working class, reality included a work life that must be combined with attending college. This aspect of their habitus led them to focus on the more pragmatic elements of earning a degree. Smith asserted that, although their approach was not valued by their teacher, students do understand the rules of the higher education field and have "decided to reformulate the game to their own advantage" (p. 432). It is clear from these examples that Bourdieu's concepts have a place in furthering the conversation around college choice as we learn more about how the ways we previously conceptualized this process are adapted by students for whom the models do not fit.

It is important to note that Bourdieu's ideas of habitus and field do not imply predetermination. Bourdieu's focus is on social systems such as education and their contribution to perpetual hierarchies in the broader society that make it difficult for people to cross class lines. It is possible, however, for individuals to choose to make decisions that move them out of their habitus. Two authors focused on this phenomenon. In Brooks's study of high school students from different levels of the middle class (2003), children at the lower levels did not want to become like their parents and consciously decided to change their social class status. Brooks noted that "young people and their parents were actively attempting to change their habitus" (p. 295). Hatcher (1998) supported this finding in his conceptual article exploring rational choice in education, arguing that for working-class students and their families, "the ability to enter into conscious strategic thinking and action is the means for overcoming the social reproductionism of their habitus" (p. 21). Importantly, Hatcher noted that decisions to attempt to span class boundaries are not single events; rather, they are "recursive" (p. 22) and many, each impacted by the immediate context and building on one another to shape larger decisions at points of transition in an individual's educational experience. The African American girls who attended a prestigious college preparatory school in Horvat and Antonio's study (1999) "pay a price" for "social mobility" (p. 339) by attempting to fit in as a means to achieving their academic aspirations. All these studies reiterate the challenges faced by students whose capital is not highly valued in educational systems as they make decisions to move out of their habitus, echoing Bloom's finding (2007) that students attempting to change their habitus face considerable risks to take advantage of the social mobility made possible by a college education.

The literature summarized above demonstrates how Bourdieu's concepts contribute to the way we think about the college choice process. Habitus and capital influence students' perceptions of the opportunities available to them, driving their practice in the fields of college choice and, for those who choose it, higher education. These lenses provide ways to explain the continued stratification in higher education and can support specific recommendations to assist students with lower access to capital in navigating the college choice process.

Chapter Summary

College choice can be described as a luxury for students from lower socioeconomic backgrounds. By no means does the assumption that they have equal access to the higher education environment that grounds most comprehensive college choice models hold true. In fact, their K–12 schooling experiences are plagued by school funding paradigms that ensure they study in the lowest-funded schools, despite the fact that they need the most help in accessing educational resources. Further, they do not have access to the same information as their middle- and upper-class peers, resulting in an inability to accurately weigh the return on their educational investments should they attend college. Limited information impedes their ability to picture themselves in a higher education environment, because they are generally less aware of the financial aid opportunities that would enable them to afford college. For low socioeconomic students, college may appear to be the way to ensure a better future, but the realities of their academic preparation, knowledge of college-going resources, and access to information keep the dream just out of reach. The result is a higher education system that is stratified by social class, with the more prestigious institutions largely populated by the upper classes, contributing to the social reproduction of social classes illustrated in Bourdieu's concepts (1977).

Pierre Bourdieu's work contributes to an understanding of how family background characteristics play into the formation of educational aspirations and expectations as well as the enactment of behaviors that lead to the fulfillment of these aspirations. This set of concepts reflects the increasing trend in college choice research to focus on issues of equity and access for both low socioeconomic students and students of color and moves the analysis of the situation away from individual students. Rather, the focus is on the social systems that do not validate the different kinds of cultural and social capital students develop in their individual habitus. Policy and practice aimed at improving the college-going rates of lower socioeconomic students must incorporate a cultural wealth paradigm that recognizes and rewards different kinds of capital. Further, Perna's model of college choice (2006), with its focus on layers of contexts, is also particularly helpful for considering the college choice processes of low socioeconomic students, for whom the factors of parental education and income, academic preparation, and educational expectations are mediated by larger school and community contexts.

For many students, social class status intersects with race and ethnicity, layering contexts of experience to further complicate their college choice processes. The literature presented in the next chapter explores the college choice experiences of students of color in an attempt to illuminate the causes of their continued underrepresentation in postsecondary education.

College Choice Processes for Students of Color

IN THE INCREASED FOCUS on issues of access and equity in higher education, many researchers have concentrated on exploring the college choice experiences of students of color. This literature recognizes that despite increases in the racial and ethnic diversity of the college-going population, proportionate increases in the participation of students of color in higher education have not materialized. Research in this area looks at early socialization experiences, the family's focus on the importance of education, K–12 schooling experiences, differential access to information about postsecondary education, perceptions of labor market rewards for higher education, and financial aid preferences. These specific foci reflect all four trends in recent research: access and equity, movement away from comprehensive models, understanding college preparation, and policy implications and impacts. Importantly, much of the research moves away from a deficit perspective in which students and their families are viewed as problems needing solutions. Rather, the focus is on how systems of education fail to adequately serve these populations of students, resulting in their lack of participation in higher education. This focus on interactions between individuals and systems when considering issues related to race in the United States shapes the discussion of literature in this chapter.

To better understand the experiences of students of color as they engage in the college choice process, the chapter begins with a summary of the extensive body of literature related to the college choice processes of students of color, engaging the literature to discuss the implications of this research for issues of access and equity for students of color. The intent is that faculty and professionals working in higher education and policymakers at many levels will find the synthesis of this literature helpful in guiding future practice, policy, and research aimed at increasing access to a range of postsecondary education opportunities for increasingly diverse college-going populations.

Research Related to the College Choice Processes of Students of Color

In the last two decades, dozens of studies have explored the topic of college choice as it relates to students from different racial and ethnic backgrounds. Some of this research is conflated with research focused on social class background, as students of color are overrepresented in lower-resource categories. The research analyzed here incorporates studies that focus exclusively on race and ethnicity as well as some that explore the intersections of class with race and ethnicity. To simplify the presentation of this literature, the studies are organized according to the three stages of Hossler and Gallagher's model (1987), which is not to imply that the research fits neatly into these categories. In fact, the experiences of students of color do not always mesh with traditional models as discussed in earlier chapters. The broad categories of predisposition, search, and choice provide an adequate organizing framework for this extensive literature base. The chapter begins with a discussion of studies focused on the formation of predispostion among students of color and their families.

Predisposition

Included in the discussion of literature related to college predisposition are studies that emphasized the formation of educational aspirations and expectations of students of color and their families. Studies examining initial behaviors enacted by students to actualize these aspirations are also included in this section. Overall, the research reviewed here illustrates that students of color share a number of elements of the predisposition phase with their white peers but that significant differences also exist.

Generally, educational aspirations and expectations play a role in the formation of predisposition, which is also true for students of color. For many years, lower postsecondary participation rates among black students were described as a result of their lower educational aspirations (Solorzano, 1992). This description reflected a deficit approach, perpetuated by the stereotype that black families do not value education. Several studies from the last two decades, however, reveal that blacks and other students of color have high educational aspirations. This finding led researchers to explore new ways to explain the gap between educational aspirations and attainment in populations of color. For example, Solorzano's study examined the effect of race, class, and gender on educational aspirations and found that blacks had higher educational attainment aspirations than whites in every socioeconomic quartile but the highest. Solorzano also noted that although a gap existed between aspirations and attainment for every racial group in his study, the gap was "much greater for Blacks than it is for Whites" (p. 33). This finding led Solorzano to posit that, because low educational aspirations are not preventing black students' enrollment in higher education, researchers must look beyond family characteristics and examine the role of schools in the aspiration-attainment gap.

Mickelson (1990) also examined the aspiration-attainment gap in black students and found that students' predisposition is based on two types of attitudes: abstract and concrete. Abstract attitudes reflect the dominant cultural ideology about higher education: that it is necessary for success in the occupational world or at the very least is a way to get ahead in that world. Concrete attitudes, formed through experiences related to the opportunity structure, have a greater bearing on behavior than abstract attitudes. The difference between dominant cultural ideals and reality becomes clearer to black students as they progress through the K–12 system so that, although they and their parents have high initial aspirations, when it comes time to decide whether to go to college, the perceived benefits do not outweigh the costs. Mickelson argued that because blacks' experiences suggest that educational payoffs in terms of occupational and other benefits are limited, their actual educational attainment is lower, despite their high aspirations. Perna's study of difference in labor market perceptions by race (2005a) confirmed this finding for Hispanic students as well.

As a result of their study, Cooper and others (1995) addressed the issue of aspirations, arguing that maintaining high aspirations throughout the college choice process was essential for college enrollment. Pitre (2006a) supported this finding, noting that although African American and white students had very similar levels of aspirations, black students were less likely to enroll in higher education. Two reasons Pitre suggested for this difference reflected other studies' findings. First, Pitre found a strong relationship between high school preparation and aspirations. Students in Pitre's study had higher educational aspirations when they believed that their high school was preparing them for college, related to Solorzano's argument (1992) that schools discourage African American students' educational goals. The relationship between college preparedness and aspirations was further illustrated by Pitre's finding (2006a) that African American students' aspirations "were not supported by the type of academic achievement that might lead to college attendance" (p. 570). This finding led to Pitre's second explanation for differences in enrollment: African American students lack information about postsecondary education, which weakens their aspirations and provides less incentive to do well academically. In a vicious cycle, Pitre posited, students whose academic achievement is lower are not targeted by high school personnel to receive information about college, further lowering their educational expectations.

Hanson's study of talent loss (1994) also explored declining aspirations by race and class. Hanson found that among students with comparable academic achievement, talent loss was more likely to occur for those with fewer resources. Because students of color often have limited access to important resources such as families with high educational attainment and positive schooling experiences, they are more likely to experience talent loss. Hanson's findings demonstrate that the impact of race is most significant as an indirect effect on access to resources, which illustrates the importance of examining the intersections of race and class.

Kao and Tienda (1998) also studied aspirations, noting that black and Hispanic students had lower aspirations than whites. These authors also found that black and Hispanic students' aspirations were not as stable over time and that family socioeconomic status played a significant role in the maintenance and actuation of those aspirations. Black and Hispanic study participants were less informed about higher education than white and Asian students, who, the authors argued, decreased their odds of "reaching their educational goals" (p. 349).

Additionally, a lack of resources disproportionately affected black and Hispanic students, while whites and Asians, in the words of the authors, "overachieved" (p. 379) without regard to their resources. Kao and Tienda echoed the calls of other researchers for increased investigation of the differences among and between racial and ethnic groups.

Another study compared aspirations of Mexican American and European American students and found that parental educational aspirations for their children change over time, weakening as their children grow older (Cooper and others, 1995). These authors suggested that it was the result of two overarching factors. First, as students advance through the educational system and become more educated than their parents, parents believe they can no longer offer effective guidance. This outcome was supported by the finding that parents with higher education levels felt more confident in their ability to provide support for their children's educational goals. Although European American parents reported higher levels of confidence than Mexican American ones, the authors noted that the low-income status of both groups contributed to low levels of confidence across the board. The second reason for the lowering of parental aspirations was that as students get closer to college-going age, parents were forced to confront the cost of postsecondary education, at which point many realized that college was beyond their financial means. The findings of this study explain why aspirations might change over time, but they also reiterate the importance of parental factors in students' predisposition, which was true also for the general literature on predisposition. These parent-related factors are explored next.

Parents' expectations shape predisposition. Hamrick and Stage (2000) found that parental expectations had the greatest direct effect on students' predisposition. Although this impact was significant for all racial and ethnic groups, it was most important for Hispanic youth and surpassed in influence only by parents' education for African American students. Another study examined the role of parents' expectations (Hao and Bonstead-Bruns, 1998) and found that interactions with parents about academic issues increased students' expectations for college. These authors also noted that when parents' and students' expectations for educational attainment were similar, students had higher levels of academic achievement. Although academic achievement differed by race and ethnicity, with Chinese and white students at the top, parents' expectations of educational attainment had a positive effect on academic achievement for all groups. Both of these studies illustrate the role of parental expectations in promoting college aspirations and show how the impact of parents' expectations varies for students from different racial and ethnic groups. These studies also found that parents' education influenced predisposition.

In Cooper and others' study (1995), parents' education had a bearing on both parents' aspirations for their children and children's college predisposition. This finding was particularly true for Mexican American families. Related to education was the lack of postsecondary information for parents in both groups. The authors reported that many parents did not know that college was required for their children's occupational goals and that even those who did hope their children would enroll in college "were unsure about application and financial aid procedures" (p. 73). Other parents were fearful about sending their children to college. In terms of ability to financially support their children's educational goals, many parents in this study expressed that immediate financial concerns were more pressing than educational goals, which resulted in few of the tangible support behaviors that Hossler and Gallagher (1987) found to be an important aspect of parental encouragement in the formation of college predisposition.

Parental expectations and education are factors in the college choice process of all students, and it is clear that they shape the formation of educational aspirations in students of color. These expectations and even the earned educations of parents of students of color, however, are mediated by social forces so that their impact is different from that of the expectations of white parents for their children. Of particular concern is the disconnect between parents' and children's aspirations and their actual educational attainment, aptly described by Hanson (1994) as "talent loss." Further explication of the factors that shape predisposition and choice for students of color illuminates the contexts that mediate this disconnect. Engagement in children's education is one of these factors.

Another parental factor in predisposition formation is engagement with children's education. In her study of Mexican American families' experiences with schooling, Delgado-Gaitan (1992) found that Mexican American parents played an essential role in socializing their children toward educational attainment. Of particular value were parents' interactions with schools, even though many parents did not feel welcome in the schools. Parents shared their own educational shortcomings with children as a way of motivating them to "take advantage" of their educational opportunities (p. 507). Like the parents in Cooper and others' study (1995), Delgado-Gaitan's parent participants often noted feeling a lack of confidence in guiding their children's education. The students in Delgado-Gaitan's study were exposed primarily to low-volume social capital in their families, with the main contribution to educational aspirations emotional support. This finding echoed Gonzales, Stoner, and Jovel's findings (2003) about the types of capital found in their Latina participants' families. Because parent engagement in their children's education is important to predisposition, it is necessary to increase these families' opportunities to engage in positive ways with schools and school personnel.

Gutman and McLoyd (2000) also looked at how parents managed their children's education, with a focus on African Americans living in poverty. They found that children of parents who used specific support strategies such as detailed conversations about education had higher academic achievement than children of parents who engaged in general support strategies. Further, when parents were more actively involved with their children's school and the broader community, their children's achievement was higher than that of children whose parents were passively involved in the school and community. Gutman and McLoyd posited that parents' own level of education affects how involved they are in their children's education, noting that parents who had positive schooling experiences are more likely to be involved with their children's school. These findings parallel those of the broader college choice literature that supports the role of parental involvement in college disposition.

Socioeconomic status also plays a role in the formation of predisposition in students of color. Hamrick and Stage (1995, 2004) examined factors in predisposition formation, disaggregating their data by racial and ethnic group. The authors found that family socioeconomic status was a significant factor in college predisposition for Hispanic, African American, and white students. For whites and Hispanics, the effect of socioeconomic status was direct, but for African American students it was indirect, affecting parental expectations and grade point average. Whether as a direct or indirect effect, socioeconomic status clearly affects predisposition. As in Hanson's study (1994), Hamrick and Stage's findings warrant further exploration of the intersection between socioeconomic status and race and ethnicity in the formation of college aspirations and illustrate the need for continued emphasis on the differences between groups of traditionally underrepresented students.

Finally, Perna (2000) examined differences in white, Hispanic, and African American decisions to attend college and found that, on average, Hispanic and African American parents are less educated than white parents, that African American and Hispanic students are more likely to attend schools with higher African American and Hispanic student populations, and that parents' involvement in educational decisions is lower for students of color than whites. In terms of the role of parents' education in college enrollment, Perna found different effects for different groups; it is less important for Hispanics than for African American and white students. The effect of social and cultural capital variables, which are related to family background characteristics, was as important in students of colors' college enrollment decisions as academic ability. Access to information was one concern Perna related to these findings, as accurate and readily available information might mediate some of the family background differences she found. Although family background and parental characteristics clearly play a complex role in college predisposition for students of color, they are not alone in the formation of educational aspirations.

As noted earlier (Pitre, 2006a; Solorzano, 1992), high school experiences influence the formation of students' educational aspirations. Several studies explored this role in depth. For some authors, the issue is students' experiences in school, while for others the concern is the structure of resources in the school itself. Lucas and Good (2001) examined what they termed "tournament track mobility" (p. 139), which occurs when students can move out of a higher track to a lower one but students in lower tracks cannot move to higher ones. These authors looked at the role of socioeconomic status and race in students' track mobility and found that blacks, Latinos, and Latinas were more likely to experience downward track mobility, meaning that tracking was occurring in schools and that students of color were more likely to move to lower tracks than whites. This finding was particularly true in heterogeneous schools, where even more evidence showed upward track mobility for white students. The nature of Lucas and Good's study did not allow them to state why tracking occurs or what its impact is, but taken with findings presented by Pitre (2006a) that students who do not feel high school is preparing them for college are less likely to enroll in college and (Perna, 2000) that academic achievement plays a role in college enrollment, one can infer that tracking has a negative effect on students' college predispositions.

Another study, qualitative in nature, examined how students accessed various levels of capital (Gonzales, Stoner, and Jovel, 2003) and found that Latinas had lower access to high-volume agents of social capital in schools than other students, limiting their college aspirations. These authors noted that capital accumulation begins in elementary schools and that students with more capital early on are able to convert that capital into additional resources as they progress through the school system. Students who do not have access to high-volume agents in schools or for whom these agents discourage postsecondary education have constrained educational choices. In fact, Gonzales, Stoner, and Jovel argued, school support for students' educational aspirations was as important as academic ability in their enrollment in college. Muhammad (2008) also emphasized the role of school support in the college aspirations of African American students, noting that African Americans' feelings of mistrust toward educational systems have grown over decades of mistreatment, which can be overcome by a "trustworthy, supportive school counselor" (p. 91). Developing a trusting relationship with students, Muhammad argued, requires that counselors provide cultural support to students, echoing Freeman's findings (1997) that cultural relevancy benefits African American students during the college choice process.

Teranishi (2002) studied the high school experiences of Chinese and Filipino students. Although Chinese students in his study reported "feeling that they were treated as a model minority, with high academic expectations placed on them by teachers and counselors" (p. 148), Filipino students experienced negative stereotypes and less support from high school personnel. Both groups of students experienced negative stereotyping, which caused internal identity conflicts that affect their educational aspirations. Teranishi's findings underline the important role of school experiences and illustrate the need to disaggregate by ethnic group when considering the experiences of students of color. Together these studies illustrate how school experiences can influence students of colors' educational aspirations. When they have little encouragement or preparation for college, students are less inclined to aspire to furthering their education. Students of color also experience schooling differently as a result of stereotypes and expectations of others based on their race and ethnicity.

Another factor in school influence on predisposition is the resources available to students of color in their schools. Solorzano and Ornelas (2004) and Teranishi, Allen, and Solorzano (2004) examined the role of high schools in creating barriers to higher education for students of color. Both studies used data from California, focusing on opportunities for students of color to enroll in Advanced Placement classes and college preparation curricula. These studies revealed that students of color attending highly segregated high schools with majority minority populations are less likely to be offered AP and other college-oriented courses than those attending schools where whites are the majority. Related to college choice, higher education options for students in the segregated high schools are limited by both their preparation and the assumptions of higher education institutions that these schools do not produce college-going students.

High school experiences affected college predisposition in the broader college choice literature, and they also factor into the aspirations of students of color. Differences exist, however, in the influence of high school on students' predispositions. The research presented here indicates that for many students of color, high school is not a place where they receive the preparation or support necessary to fulfill their educational aspirations. Lack of support, fewer college preparatory classes, environments that do not support college attendance, and information are barriers students of color face in the college choice process. Not only do schools often fail to mediate the impact of these barriers; students of color also report that the barriers are frequently exacerbated by their interactions with school personnel. Given the problematic nature of their school experiences, for many students of color peers become an important element of forming aspirations.

Azmitia and Cooper (2001) explored the impact of peers on Latino and white students' academic achievement and educational aspirations. Students reported that peers were considered both challenges and resources to educational achievement and aspirations. These authors found that both white and Latino students relied on peers more than families as resources, but students reported that peers also posed more challenges to their educational achievement and aspirations than their families. Differences were found between the role of peers for students in regular high school classes and their peers in a college preparatory program. Students in the college preparatory program reported a higher degree of challenge from peers than those in the regular high school program, which may indicate that peers can be a detriment to students' college-going plans. Azmitia and Cooper noted that future research should involve comparative studies of peer influence between students from different racial and ethnic backgrounds. Gibson, Gandara, and Koyama (2004) also explored the role of peers in Mexican American youths' schooling experiences and found that peers fill in for family when college knowledge is needed and the family is unable to provide it. Peers also play an essential role in establishing a "sense of belonging" (p. 11), which is connected to academic motivation and achievement. Gibson, Gandara, and Koyama argued that this belonging is particularly important for students of Mexican origin, who often do not feel comfortable in their high school environments, especially when they are in the minority. Azmitia and Cooper (2001) and Gibson, Gandara, and Koyama (2004) both provide evidence that peers play a role in educational achievement and aspirations. Another group of studies focused on information networks and how students of color use such networks in the college choice process.

Information networks played a role in the educational experiences of students of color in studies by Stanton-Salazar and Dornbusch (1995) and Stanton-Salazar and Spina (2000). The earlier study focused on students of Mexican origin and found that students with higher grades and aspirations tended to have higher levels of social and cultural capital than those with lower achievement and aspirations. Family socioeconomic status was an important source of capital but so were language and peers; students from higher socioeconomic backgrounds had peers with more capital, which tended to reinforce their educational aspirations. Stanton-Salazar's later work with Spina (2000) focused more broadly on resilient youth. These authors noted that students of color operate in a dominant ideology that leads to "marginality" and "cultural conflict" (p. 242) and argued that "supportive agents" (p. 244), including peers, can help students overcome barriers to the formation of complex and multiple identities that allow them to function in several cultural milieus. Peers and other agents assist students by providing support, helping them navigate multiple cultural systems, and nurturing the development of networks that support them as they move through educational systems. Stanton-Salazar and Spina also noted the negative influence of network factors such as "racially segregated neighborhoods, assimilationist ideological forces, demoralizing school environments, or disaffected youth subcultures" (p. 247) in the educational progress of students of color. The work of Stanton-Salazar and his colleagues set the stage for other studies exploring the impact of networks on the college choice processes of Latina and Latino students.

Two studies expanded the understanding of how networks of peers and other significant agents influence the predisposition of Latina and Latino students (Perez and McDonough, 2008; Person and Rosenbaum, 2006). Person and Rosenbaum found that chain networks have both positive and negative effects on the college choice process and that Latina and Latino students rely more on chain enrollment networks, defined as postsecondary information from family and friends, than do other students. Although these networks may encourage participation in college in ways that impersonal interactions do not, these authors found that students who rely exclusively on chain networks, particularly information from peers and relatives already enrolled in college, have access to less complete information than students who look outside their network for information. Given the role of accurate information in both the formation of predisposition and the search and choice process, limited information has a negative influence on students' aspirations and enrollment. Further, Person and Rosenbaum argued, on-campus enclaves that result from chain enrollment networks can limit students' access to information and services that enhance their success once they enroll. Perez and McDonough also found that Latina and Latino students relied extensively on extended networks of family and peers in the formation of their college aspirations. Supporting Person and Rosenbaum's notion that these networks have both positive and negative roles in the process, Perez and McDonough argued that college preparation models should validate the community orientation of Latina and Latino students, using community resources that families can access and targeting individual families and peer groups to ensure that Latina and Latino students and their families have adequate information regarding postsecondary education opportunities.

It is evident that college predisposition for students of color is different from that of white students. Students of color face significant barriers to forming college predisposition as a result of inequitable educational settings and social and cultural factors that mediate and dilute their initial high educational aspirations. Their access to information is further constrained for a number of reasons, including their families' understanding of college-going processes, how they are tracked in high school, and how they use peer and family networks as information sources. In terms of cultural wealth, family and community play significant roles in aiding students as they engage in behaviors that lead to the fulfillment of their aspirations, despite societal barriers. This role increases as students move into the search and choice phases of the college choice process, which is the focus of the next section.

Search and Choice

During the search and choice stage of the college choice process (Hossler and Gallagher, 1987), students use information and consult peers, family, and high school and higher education sources as they define their choice set, narrow it to reasonable options, and make decisions of where to apply and enroll. Hossler and Gallagher's model assumes that students have equal access to information, but throughout this monograph, evidence has shown that students of color access information in different ways and in quantitatively different amounts, which affects their enrollment decisions. This section explores in more detail the research related to the search and choice phase of the process, with a focus on how parental and family background characteristics, cost, availability of financial aid, access to information, and academic preparation and high school context shape this process for students of color.

Two family-related factors have a significant impact on the enrollment of students of color in college: parents' education and family income, and family involvement in children's educational endeavors. Before examining the studies related to these factors, it is important to note that both Tierney (2002) and Knight, Norton, Bentley, and Dixon (2004) argued that for many communities of color, the traditional definition of the family is not sufficient to describe the extended network of individuals who play a significant role in the development of enrollment plans for students of color. Knight, Norton, Bentley, and Dixon noted that "a reconceptualization of family versus parent involvement can be implemented in family-school partnerships that respect, understand, and utilize the multiple interpersonal relationships through which students find support" (p. 116). Tierney also suggested a redefinition of parental involvement, expanding the understanding of the many individuals who are part of the academic success of a student of color. Some of the studies described below incorporate these broader views of the family, while others rely on parental factors only; however, both have value in illustrating how students of color move through the search and choice process.

Among the most commonly emphasized parental factors in students' predisposition are parent income and education. Lopez-Turley, Santos, and Ceja (2007) noted that although parents' income remains important, in their study of changes in enrollment patterns from 1972 to 1992, parents' education became increasingly important. Both of these factors, the authors argued, play a role in the development of "opportunity expectations" (p. 1213) that influence whether students apply to selective colleges and universities. Lower income and less education for parents correlate with the lower likelihood of applying to more selective institutions. Additionally, the participation of students of color in these types of institutions dropped over Lopez-Turley, Santos, and Ceja's study period. Hallinan (2000) supported Lopez-Turley, Santos, and Ceja's findings, noting that parental income and education influence student achievement, which then affects institutional choice. Further, Hallinan argued, schools perpetuate these differences in achievement. Finally, Kao and Thompson's review of literature exploring racial and ethnic stratification in higher education (2003) found that parents' education and income were "the best predictor of eventual academic outcomes among youth" (p. 431), noting that Hispanic parents have the lowest education and Asian parents the highest (although differences exist among ethnic groups in the Asian category). These authors also attempted to show how these differences played out as students selected institutions; overall, Hispanic students were far more likely to attend community colleges or less prestigious institutions than Asian students.

In sum, this research posits that students of color face barriers to higher education enrollment because of the lower education status of their parents and the fact that they come disproportionately from lower-income households. Recognizing these barriers illustrates how comprehensive college choice models may not be appropriate for students of color.

Although parents' education and income play a clear part in the enrollment decisions of students of color, parents' involvement is also a factor. For example, Perna and Titus (2005) found that parents' involvement was positively related to students' enrollment in college but that the impact of this involvement varied by racial and ethnic group. The authors categorized involvement in two ways: parents engage actively with their children in discussing and planning for their postsecondary education, and parents are involved with the school. For all students, parents' involvement with the school was an important predictor of college enrollment, but only when that involvement was positive. When parents' involvement with the schools was centered on students' behavioral issues or academic struggles, probability of college enrollment dropped. In terms of student-parent involvement, the "college enrollment 'premium' is smaller for African Americans than for high school graduates of other groups" (p. 505). These authors equated involvement to social capital and posited that some of the effect is explained by differences in habitus. Like Hallinan (2000), Perna and Titus noted that schools play a role in how this parental factor affects enrollment. African Americans and Hispanics are more likely to attend schools with fewer resources and where generally fewer parents are in contact with the school in ways that positively affect enrollment. Perna and Titus found that students of color were more sensitive to the cost of higher education, with African Americans being the most sensitive. Because sensitivity to cost is related to parents' income, the authors pointed out, parental education plays an indirect role in price sensitivity because of its impact on income. The influence of costs and financial aid in students' search and choice process is examined next.

Studies that examine the impact of costs and financial aid in college choice focus on two specific aspects: sensitivity to the cost of higher education and the role of financial aid in mitigating that sensitivity. Underlying many of these studies is the recognition that information about costs and availability of aid is not equally accessible to students from all backgrounds. Misinformation about costs and availability of aid is a significant issue for students of color. Also of importance in the conversation about financial aid is type of aid. Some authors argued that the recent trend toward dependency on loans in federal- and state-based aid discourages students of color from going to college.

Paulsen and St. John's research (2002) related to the financial nexus focused on social class, but within the social class categories established for their study, students of color were disproportionately represented in the low- and low-middle-income range, allowing the authors to generate some conclusions regarding the role of financial aid in the enrollment of students of color. By looking at data on persistence, the authors surmised that many low-income students, who did not choose their institutions based on available aid, were not aware of the financial aid available. This factor, combined with what the authors term "an alarmingly high sensitivity to tuition" (p. 219) led them to argue that even low-tuition institutions may pose too much of a burden for low-income students. In terms of financial aid, the authors found that both grants and loans had a negative impact on low-income students' persistence, which they argued indicated that "both forms of aid were inadequate" (p. 229) and that the high tuition–high aid trend does not benefit low-income students. Paulsen and St. John's work touched on several important points for students of color, who were disproportionately represented in the lower-income categories of this study. First, students in these groups are extremely sensitive to cost as they decide which college to attend. Second, they are relatively unaware of the financial aid that is available, so even though they tend to choose institutions where the costs are lower, they often take on a burden they cannot bear. Finally, if the trend toward larger loans and smaller grants has a negative impact on the persistence decisions of these students, it may also affect their initial enrollment choices.

Related to availability of financial aid is that students of color are more sensitive to cost and the availability of financial aid than white students (Heller, 1999; Ikenberry and Hartle, 1998; Kim, 2004; McPherson and Shapiro, 1991). Other research specifically exploring the institutional choice processes of students of color also found that cost matters. Kurlaender's work (2006) explored the high representation of Latina and Latino students in community colleges and posited that lower socioeconomic status factored into this phenomenon; because many Latina and Latino students come from a lower socioeconomic background, community colleges represent an attractive choice that better fits their financial constraints. Freeman's study of African American high school students (1997) reiterated the impact of cost on students' choices. A central theme of her study was that economic barriers are a salient aspect of students' choice processes. These barriers come in the form of concerns about ability to pay as well as issues of lost income resulting from the decision to pursue higher education rather than work.

The trend toward loan-based financial aid was one explanation Hauser and Anderson (1991) suggested for the decline in enrollment of African American students between 1976 and 1986. These authors argued that because black families are more "vulnerable to unemployment" (p. 275) and have less wealth than whites, they are less able to shoulder loans, noting that "a potential post-college debt of $10,000 would loom much larger for blacks, regardless of their family's current income, than for whites" (p. 275). Another way both cost and availability of aid shape enrollment decisions of students of color is in their perceptions of labor market conditions, which, as Perna (2006), Freeman (1997), and Mickelson (1990) found, influences their aspirations. Specifically, if students and their families expect a low return on their educational investment, they are less likely to take out loans to make the initial investment than a student who perceives that the potential payoff of an education is higher.

Finally, geographic location seems to be a significant factor in institutional choice processes of students of color. Grodsky (2002) found that Latina and Latino students are more apt to select institutions that are close to home, which Stewart and Post (1990) found was also true for blacks, Asians, and Native Americans in their study. Kurlaender (2006) speculated that one reason for the high presence of Latina and Latino students in community colleges is their preference for institutions closer to home. Smith's participants (2007) chose institutions closer to home for cost reasons but also because they were more familiar with these institutions, which eased the transition to college. McDonough, Antonio, and Trent (1997) found that African American students who attended historically black colleges and universities were highly mobile, again emphasizing the importance of fit over more pragmatic institutional factors. Overall, students of color consider location an important factor in the institutional choice process.

Cost and availability of financial aid weigh heavily in the search and choice process of students of color (Hurtado, Inkelas, Briggs, and Rhee, 1997). Despite their importance to the postsecondary decision-making process, some authors (Ikenberry and Hartle, 1998; Paulsen and St. John, 2002) reported that students of color and their families are less informed than white middle-class students about postsecondary opportunities generally and about costs and financial aid specifically. Lack of access to information is a common thread that runs through several studies that explored the barriers to college enrollment for students of color.

Information is a significant factor in the search and choice process for any student, but evidence suggests that students of color do not access information about college opportunities and financial aid in the same ways that white students do. For example, African American students are more likely to rely on high school personnel for information, particularly when their parents have not been to college (Plank and Jordan, 2001). This situation is problematic because high school personnel frequently do not contribute positively to college-going processes of students of color (Freeman, 1997; Immerwahr, 2003). Teranishi (2002) found differences in access to information across Asian Pacific Americans, and Gonzales, Stoner, and Javel (2003) reported that Latinas did not have ready access to high-volume capital agents such as counselors in their schools. As a result, Immerwahr (2003) states, these students "risk making pivotal, life-changing decisions based on inadequate and sometimes misleading information" (p. 15). Although lack of information is one challenge students of color face, academic preparation is another.

Academic preparation affects the types of institutions to which students can apply. Students whose preparation has not put them on the college track may not apply to college at all, while others find their options limited to community colleges (Hurtado, Inkelas, Briggs, and Rhee, 1997). Gonzales, Stoner, and Jovel (2003) argued that Latinas were overrepresented in special education classes and were often mistakenly assigned to ESL courses, both of which inhibited their ability to take college preparatory classes. Hispanic students in Immerwahr's study (2003) found that teachers frequently did not support their postsecondary interests. African American students in Freeman's study (1999) described loss of hope as one result of this treatment in schools. Hurtado, Inkelas, Briggs, and Rhee (1997) and Teranishi (2002) noted that students who were identified early as academic achievers were more likely to receive support and information from school personnel, underlining the importance of equitable educational opportunities for all students. High school context plays a role in enrollment choices as well. The schools students of color attend are more likely to have fewer resources, meaning that resources are limited for college guidance counseling, particularly if the school does not have a culture of sending students to college (Rowan-Kenyon, Bell, and Perna, 2008). Additionally, tracking factored into the enrollment process for students of color in the work of Immerwahr (2003) and Lucas and Good (2001). These studies reveal a number of barriers students of color must overcome as they navigate the college choice process.

Although many studies focus on barriers, Gandara's stories of Chicano students' success (1999) highlight the positive influence of four factors on their educational journeys. A focus on literacy, often in Spanish, was the first. Reading was an important activity in the homes of the students in Gandara's study, but these families also emphasized ideas and information as well as inquiry. Second, the successful students in Gandara's study attended desegregated schools with access to social capital, friendships with white students, and the development of "cultural flexibility" (p. 46). This finding aligns with Stanton-Salazar and Spina's work (2000), which emphasized the development of cultural competence in several different cultural worlds. Third, these successful Chicano students embodied a value of hard work and a belief that "effort was more important than ability in achieving academic goals" (p. 46). Finally, participants' families told stories of hope. Although not all the stories were entirely factual, Gandara proposed that they motivated students as well as served as a form of cultural capital with a habitus of education, "self-worth, competence, and hopefulness" (p. 50). Such stories counter the hopelessness the African American students in Freeman's study (1999) expressed as they moved through educational systems that did not understand or validate their cultural backgrounds.

It is evident that students of color experience the college choice process in ways that are different from white students. The research synthesized above paints a picture of challenges to the successful navigation of educational systems, lack of support and information, and growing concerns about the costs and benefits of going to college. Yet many students of color do successfully navigate the college choice process and enroll in a range of higher education institutions. To ensure that more students of color are able to attain their goals, it is necessary to continue to explore the practices, policies, and research that aid and hinder this process.

Chapter Summary

The story presented in this chapter is one of unrealized aspirations. Students of color and their families highly value education, and in their early years aspirations are high. Yet over time, the combination of schools with limited resources, lack of support from school personnel, inadequate access to information about postsecondary opportunity generally and financial aid resources in particular, social forces that communicate low returns on educational investments, and tracking into nonacademic high school courses discourages these students from fulfilling their initial expectations. The college choice literature related to the experiences of students of color illustrates continued residential and educational segregation that leads one to believe that not much progress has been made since schools were desegregated nearly two generations ago. Although individual success stories do exist, the overall picture explains all too clearly the numbers presented earlier, illustrating the continued stratification of higher education.

As a result of this evidence, the college choice field clearly calls for attention to individual student needs, moving away from aggregated understandings of the college choice process to recognition of the complex, nuanced navigational experiences of students of color. The literature presented in this chapter illustrates this movement. Continued racial stratification in higher education motivates this attention, and although progress is certainly being made, clearly more exploration is needed before we can understand and begin to systematically address the issues through policy and practice. Bourdieu's framework (1977, 1987, 1993) and the cultural wealth paradigm (Villalpando and Solorzano, 2005) can assist in unpacking the numerous issues raised in this chapter around the college choice processes of students of color. Both paradigms move away from examining the shortcomings of students and their families that illustrate deficit thinking and move toward systemic and cultural critiques that highlight the barriers students of color face as they make postsecondary decisions. Paralleling the trend away from comprehensive college choice models in the general college choice field, this chapter illuminates how the assumptions of equal access to information, adequate academic preparation, and financial resources that provide the foundations for most comprehensive models do not hold true for students of color.

By organizing the literature around Hossler and Gallagher's three-stage model (1987), evidence of the differences between white students and students of color as well as between different groups of students of color was revealed. Inequities exist for students of color at all stages of the process, leading in sum to their lower participation in higher education. The picture painted here depicts a dismal failure for the dominant ideology that education is the great social equalizer. Moving away from deficit models and incorporating the cultural wealth perspective enhances the ability of professionals, policymakers, and researchers to adequately explain and begin to address persistent inequities in higher education. The following chapter ties the extensive body of research presented in this monograph together, highlighting existing programs and policies that work to remedy the differential participation of students of color and low socioeconomic students in higher education.

College Preparation Programs

UNDERSTANDING COLLEGE CHOICE PROCESSES is essential for higher education researchers and professionals interested in increasing access and persistence in college. Changing demographics across the United States lead to a call for a renewed commitment to equity in higher education, and many programs and practices seek to increase the participation of underrepresented students in postsecondary education. Creating links between a theoretical understanding of how students choose whether and where to attend college and the practices that enhance their decision making can contribute to higher completion rates across the many student populations higher education institutions serve. This chapter focuses on these links among research, policy, and practice. To develop these links, several existing programs geared toward increasing college participation rates are outlined, using an organizing framework suggested by Corwin, Colyar, and Tierney (2005). The chapter ends with a discussion of the value of the cultural wealth paradigm (Villalpando and Solorzano, 2005) for developing college preparatory programs.

College Preparation and Access Programs

Although enrollments in higher education have increased in the last twenty years, it is clear that racial and social class stratification continue to plague the higher education arena. In response to the continued low participation of students of color and low socioeconomic status students in postsecondary education, policymakers and professionals have developed a variety of outreach and preparation programs intended to assist students who otherwise might not access higher education in earning college degrees. These programs exist at federal and state levels, at higher education institutions, in K–12 schools, and under the purview of community or private organizations. The following sections provide background information on the development of these programs and then describe some of the more widely known programs in an effort to illustrate how research has driven the formation of college preparation programs to date.

Overview of College Preparation and Access Programs

Federal college preparation programs sprouted up in the 1960s. Upward Bound was the first, and Talent Search and Student Support services were added as part of the 1965 Higher Education Act (Swail and Perna, 2002). These programs, known as TRIO, were intended to serve students who faced both economic and educational barriers to continuing their education into college. The most recent federal college preparation program is Gaining Early Awareness and Readiness for Undergraduate Programs (GEAR UP), which was created as part of the Higher Education Act's 1998 reauthorization. GEAR UP consists of partnerships between K–12 schools, higher education institutions, and community organizations. Federal programs play an important role in the college preparation program landscape; however, because they have specific target populations, they fall short of providing access to information and preparation for the vast majority of students. In light of this shortfall, a number of nongovernmental programs have emerged to bridge the gap.

Examples of nongovernmental programs include Mathematics, Engineering, Science Achievement (MESA), established by University of California engineering faculty and high school science teachers in the 1970s; High School Puente, also established in California, with a goal of increasing the four-year college enrollment of students, particularly Latinas and Latinos; Advancement via Individual Determination (AVID), developed in 1981 and targeting middle-range students who do not qualify for federal or merit-based college preparation programs; I Have a Dream (IHAD), founded by Eugene Lang and now funded by the I Have a Dream Foundation; and Neighborhood Academic Initiative (NAI), a partnership between the University of Southern California and Los Angeles high schools that serve predominantly students of color.

Many other similar programs exist, but these specific programs are among the most notable and widely recognized committed to preparing students for college. Most of these programs incorporate early interventions such as academic counseling, mentoring, and academic preparation for college. Some include funding incentives, scholarships, and other sources of support once students enter the higher education environment. Many programs promote the development of supportive peer and family networks to assist students in planning for and attaining their educational goals. Most nongovernmental programs receive funding from private foundations as well as government entities such as the TRIO programs and the National Science Foundation. These programs serve thousands of students across the United States; however, it is clear from the research on college choice presented in this monograph that their efforts have not alleviated the stratification in higher education.

State programs and policies have also joined the effort to increase the enrollment of a range of students in higher education. State programs often emphasize financial support. Notable is Georgia's Helping Outstanding Pupils Educationally (HOPE) program, a merit-based aid program that covers the cost of tuition, fees, and books if a student attends a public state institution or pays $3,000 toward an in-state private college education. Similar programs exist in a number of states. Other state initiatives emphasize a K–16 approach to education, attempting to ease the transition between high school and college. The Stanford Bridge Project (Kirst and Bracco, 2004) was established to provide a better understanding of programs embracing the K–16 approach; it focused on three areas in its assessment of such programs: postsecondary admissions policies, college placement and advising policies in both two- and four-year institutions, and state-level policies focused on K–12 and higher education (p. 4). The Stanford researchers evaluated programs in several states and found mixed results regarding their effectiveness.

This brief overview demonstrates the vast array of programs and policies geared toward improving participation in higher education across a range of diverse cultural, educational, and social class backgrounds. Rather than provide a detailed discussion of such programs (see Fenske, Geranios, Keller, and Moore [1997]), the following sections use a framework for effective college preparation programs proposed by Corwin, Colyar, and Tierney (2005) to organize a brief description of several predominant programs designed to increase access to higher education for students of color and low socioeconomic status students.

A Framework for Effective Programs

In response to the continued concern about the underrepresentation of students of color and low socioeconomic students in higher education, Corwin, Colyar, and Tierney (2005) reflected on curricular and cocurricular elements of programs designed to increase access to higher education and their potential contribution to addressing the issue. The authors argued that nine characteristics are important, if not essential, to developing successful programs (p. 3):

An emphasis on the culture of the student

Family engagement

Incorporation of peer groups

Early, structured intervention—no later than ninth grade—with consistent structure

Counselors who exhibit knowledge and are available to students

Access to college preparation curricula

Little to no emphasis on cocurricular activities

Mentoring

Results that can be achieved at a reasonable cost

Some components such as family engagement, early intervention, and college preparation curricula are essential to successful programs, while others (mentoring, peer groups, cultural emphasis), the authors argued, are helpful but not necessary. What is important, however, is that through these components, programs focus on developing the intellectual skills necessary for college and communicate them to students by building a "cultural scaffolding" (p. 4) that emphasizes students' cultural backgrounds. The intellectual skills essential to a college preparation program include academic preparation, access to information and college-going strategies, aspirations and the self-efficacy needed to fulfill them, socialization strategies, and a working knowledge of financial aid and financial planning. These intellectual skills and the concept of cultural scaffolding together provide the organizing framework for the following review of current college preparation programs.

Essential Components of College Preparation: A Review of Several Current Programs

This review of college preparation programs focuses on seven programs representing a range of federally supported and private or locally funded efforts to increase access to college: TRIO, GEAR UP, AVID, MESA, IHAD, NAI, and Puente. These programs are widely recognized for their endeavors, and although the list is not exhaustive, it represents a cross-section of opportunities that illustrate the connections between research and practice. The programs are briefly introduced below and then compared across the elements of Corwin, Colyar, and Tierney's framework (2005).

The TRIO programs (Upward Bound, Talent Search, and Student Support Services) were developed in the 1960s to "provide supplementary academic support to low-income, historically underrepresented students" (Swail, 2000, p. 89). In the 1980s, the Ronald E. McNair Postbaccalaureate Achievement Program was added to the TRIO umbrella. These federal government–funded programs target low-income first-generation students across the United States and provide year-round services. Upward Bound is the oldest of the TRIO programs, offering supplemental instruction to low socioeconomic status, first-generation students in on-campus summer programs. Talent Search focuses on younger students, grades six through twelve, providing information about college opportunities as well as financial aid, scholarships, and admissions processes. Student Support Services and the McNair program emphasize college persistence and continuation into graduate school rather than access to college. Taken together, the TRIO programs assist students through a progression of steps to attain their educational goals.

GEAR UP, another federal program, was initiated in 1998. Although GEAR UP shares many elements of the TRIO programs, its defining characteristics are its cohort approach and requirement that schools, higher education institutions, and community entities partner to support the educational advancement of students (Swail, 2000). The idea behind the partnership is to provide students with an integrated experience that increases college awareness and aspirations as well as information about financial planning for college (Cabrera and others, 2006). GEAR UP focuses on involving both students and their families and includes visits to campus, summer camps, information sessions with higher education representatives, career planning, and academic preparation.

AVID was first established in California in the early 1980s by Mary Catherine Swanson, a high school teacher, in partnership with the University of California, San Diego. AVID targets students of color and low socioeconomic students by making a college preparatory curriculum available to them. The focus is on a rigorous curriculum; AVID students enroll in Advanced Placement and other college preparatory classes in their regular high school and participate in an AVID classroom one period a day, where they are taught the skills necessary to manage the higher expectations of their college preparatory classes. AVID is an example of a program that has expanded beyond its local beginnings, serving more than three hundred thousand students in more than four thousand high schools across the United States and internationally. AVID is primarily funded through contributions from organizations and individuals.

IHAD was founded by Eugene Lang, who, when visiting his elementary school alma mater, promised any sixth grade student who completed high school and went on to college a full-tuition scholarship. The IHAD program has expanded to more than two hundred programs across the United States, with a commitment to continued early intervention. Programs start no later than the sixth grade, allowing a significant impact on the formation of educational aspirations. The program emphasizes financial assistance and involves parents as mentors and leaders for group activities. IHAD also uses personal "sponsors" (Fenske, Geranios, Keller, and Moore, 1997) to provide financial support for students and develop personal relationships with students that support them through the duration of the college choice process.

In 1970 the University of California created the MESA program to "develop academic and leadership skills, raise educational expectations, and instill confidence in students from backgrounds historically underrepresented in fields such as engineering, physical science, and other math-based fields" (Fashola and Slavin, 1997, p. 29). The Mesa Schools Program (MSP) is the main vehicle for reaching these goals, providing middle and high school students with the academic assistance needed to achieve success in science and math fields. Additional offerings include math, science, and test preparation workshops, college advising, curriculum planning, campus visits, summer programs, and skill development classes. To be eligible for the MSP, students must be high achieving and interested in math and science.

An example of a high school–university partnership is the Neighborhood Academic Initiative (NAI), which annually enrolls about forty seventh grade students who commit to staying in the program through their high school graduation. Most students in the program are African American or Hispanic, are primarily first-generation college students, and are not necessarily high performers academically. Daily before school, students attend English and math classes at the University of Southern California taught by local high school teachers hired by NAI. At a "Saturday Enrichment Academy" (Tierney and Jun, 2001, p. 212), high school students learn computer, social, and study skills. Parents are required to attend Saturday sessions that focus on how families can support students in college. Students who complete the program, apply to, and are admitted to the University of Southern California receive full tuition from the university. NAI prides itself on the use of a "cultural integrity" model, reflecting the cultural wealth perspective.

Puente emphasizes college preparation for students from populations typically underrepresented in higher education, with an emphasis on Latina and Latino students. The program was founded by two high school teachers, Felix Galaviz and Patricia McGrath, who had a vision to improve the college-going rates of Latina and Latino students. Addressing needs in the areas of rigorous instruction in writing, intensive and consistent counseling, and mentoring, the program is housed in more than thirty California high schools and has shown success in increasing Latina and Latino students' participation in higher education (Gandara, 2002). Mentors and counselors provide students with access to essential college planning and preparation information, while the academic elements of the program increase their ability to succeed in higher education.

These programs represent a variety of approaches to increasing the enrollment of students of color and low socioeconomic status in higher education. They demonstrate that individuals, schools, higher education institutions, and the federal government all have roles to play in increasing access to higher education. They also illustrate the many facets required for making progress in this direction. The following section relates these programs to Corwin, Colyar, and Tierney's framework (2005) for effective college preparation programs.

Measuring Up: Comparing Existing Programs with the Essential Components Framework

Essential components of college preparation programs, according to Corwin, Colyar, and Tierney (2005), contribute to the development of an intellectual scaffolding and a cultural scaffolding (p. 4). The intellectual scaffolding comprises foundations such as academic preparation, access to information necessary for planning and strategies for using that information, educational aspirations and the development of the self-efficacy needed to attain educational goals, socialization and acculturation strategies, and a working knowledge of financial aid and financial planning. The cultural scaffolding incorporates a cultural wealth approach, relying on the strengths and networks students bring with them, and framing skill attainment in a way that "does not impinge on a student's cultural background" (p. 6). Each element is presented in more detail in the following paragraphs describing how these programs incorporate these essential components.

Academic preparation includes involvement in a rigorous college preparatory curriculum. Perna (2005b) argued that academic preparation is particularly important for lower socioeconomic students. Because many of the programs described above target the college enrollment of students from low-income backgrounds, academic preparation is an essential component of college preparation programs. Noting that labels such as "academic or college preparation track" (p. 116) can be misleading because of variations in the intensity and quality of such tracks across high schools, Perna argued that an "accurate definition of academic preparation describes the quality and quantity of courses" taken (p. 117). According to Perna, subject areas that have the most impact on college attendance are math, science, and foreign language. Corwin, Colyar, and Tierney (2005) noted that a college preparatory curriculum was the most important aspect of a college preparation program, so one would expect to find this component in most programs.

In different ways, all the programs described above incorporate some emphasis on academic preparedness. In fact, all of the programs except IHAD have specific academic preparation elements. Upward Bound provides students with supplemental instruction and the opportunity to attend academically rigorous classes on higher education campuses in its summer programs. AVID and NAI students take classes intended to improve their study and technological skills, and both groups are enrolled in "college preparatory" classes; AVID students take Advanced Placement and honors courses in their high schools, and NAI students enroll in courses taught at the University of Southern California. MESA also has a college preparatory element. In addition to the Mesa Schools Program study skills workshops, the program's minimum math requirement feeds directly into the definition of academic preparation set out by Perna (2005b). Puente exposes students to college preparatory classes through its academic preparedness component and focus on rigorous writing courses. Although IHAD encourages students to engage in an academically rigorous curriculum through the early establishment of college aspirations, no formal structure provides it in the program. Colwin, Colyar, and Tierney's framework for college preparation programs suggests that all such programs incorporate academic preparedness elements. Additionally, Perna (2005b) and Adelman (2006) might recommend that an increased focus on math, science, and foreign language would enhance future programs intended to increase the participation of underrepresented students in higher education.

The second element of college preparation programs (Colwin, Colyar, and Tierney (2005) is *access to information about higher education and strategies to use that information to reach educational goals*. This element stresses that not only is access to information important but also that students need the skills to process the information and make decisions based on it. The authors stress the key role of family and other networks in assisting students with information processing and decision making. Further, the role of mentors who can aid students through the admissions and financial aid application processes contributes to this program element.

As seen in previous chapters, access to adequate information is a key component of the college choice process, and the importance of this element is reflected in the college preparation programs described previously. All of them incorporate information gathering and processing in their structure. AVID, NAI, Upward Bound, and Puente are explicit in their focus on developing students' ability to process information, and GEAR UP's integrated approach ensures exposure to a range of information sources. IAHD uses sponsors and parents to assist students in gathering and processing information, while MESA uses workshop settings for this purpose. Given evidence that limited access to information is a barrier for both students of color and low socioeconomic status students, future college preparation programs should also incorporate means of information gathering and processing. Additionally, the cultural wealth perspective would urge these programs to involve extended family networks in this process.

College-going aspirations and self-efficacy are also essential in college preparation programs (Corwin, Colyar, and Tierney, 2005). The research outlined earlier in this monograph indicates that educational aspirations play an important role in students' college choice process. Yet for students of color and low-income students, a gap exists between aspirations and attainment. The self-efficacy aspect of this program component might help alleviate some of the talent loss described in the research. Nora (2002) reiterated the importance of self-efficacy in students' college choice processes and persistence patterns. In this case, self-efficacy is conceptualized as students' ability to set goals, plan for, and actualize their educational aspirations.

Several of the programs described above attend to developing college aspirations and self-efficacy, even though they may not describe their efforts explicitly as such. For example, IHAD and Talent Search both focus on influencing the formation of young students' educational aspirations. Working with youth, beginning in elementary and middle school, allows these programs to assist students in early curricular planning that sets a path for their academic achievement, which, according to the college choice research, contributes to their likelihood of going to college. Puente focuses specifically on assisting students in the development of goal-setting, planning, and decision-making skills that are necessary not only to complete the college choice process but also for their success in college. AVID's use of a specific classroom in which information-processing and decision-making skills are taught provides a safe space for students to challenge themselves and a supportive network of peers and teachers who are invested in their success, which contributes to a sense of self-efficacy. NAI refers to its students as "scholars" from the beginning of their participation in the program to develop a sense of self-efficacy and confidence in their academic abilities. And the MESA program focuses on developing science- and math-specific skills and building students' confidence. All of these efforts to build self-efficacy contribute to the maintenance of high educational aspirations that several researchers noted was important to resolving the gap between aspirations and attainment.

The *cultural scaffolding* element of college preparation programs is significant (Corwin, Colyar, and Tierney, 2005). Recognizing the distinctive aspects of students' backgrounds that serve as supports throughout the college choice process and into their college endeavors is the focus. Extended family networks, language abilities, peer groups, and cultural values of education are all part of the package students bring with them to the college choice process. Cultural scaffolding relates to the ideas of cultural wealth (Villalpando and Solorzano, 2005), and an emphasis on this area reflects the call of current research to consider the needs of individual students rather than to think of them as pieces that fit into comprehensive models.

The Puente, AVID, and NAI programs place the highest value on students' cultural backgrounds. All three of these programs recognize that students come to the process with various support networks and values that enhance their ability to achieve their educational goals. These three programs, while structured and consistent across students, also place students first, providing extensive one-on-one interaction with mentors, counselors, and teachers who can assist students in navigating the college choice process in ways that are consistent with their cultural backgrounds and values. Parents and families are encouraged, if not required, to participate in these programs alongside students, which increases their ability to support students' educational endeavors. These approaches to cultural scaffolding mesh well with the field's trend toward understanding and acting on a better sense of different students' experiences of the college choice process. This focus, the research tells us, is necessary if we are to address the ongoing inequities in the participation of students of color and low socioeconomic students in higher education.

The final component of the intellectual scaffolding in Corwin, Colyar, and Tierney's framework is *financial aid and financial planning*. Given the research focus on the lack of information students of color, low socioeconomic students, and their families have about the cost of higher education and the availability of financial aid, it is clear that it is an essential element of any college preparation program intended to increase the college enrollment of students from these groups. Corwin, Colyar, and Tierney highlight the negative impact that a lack of information about financing college can have on students' enrollment patterns, but they also note that students and their families need more information regarding the eventual returns on the investment of a college education. This focus reflects other researchers' concerns about labor market perceptions' negatively influencing enrollment decisions for students of color (Mickelson, 1990; Perna, 2006).

The significance of this element is reflected in the fact that all the college preparation programs incorporate financial coaching. IHAD provides students with the financial resources necessary to attend college, and NAI offers a financial incentive to students who attend the University of Southern California. For students who go out of state, however, NAI provides extensive support through the financial planning and financial aid application process. NAI, Puente, IHAD, MESA, and AVID all seek family involvement in students' educational planning, so everyone gains a clear understanding of the benefits and costs of higher education as well as the resources available to help defray those costs. The TRIO programs emphasize assisting students with the financial planning element of the college choice process. Given the current high tuition–high aid environment, coaching underserved students and their families through the financial aspects of college enrollment is a key component of any college preparation program.

Chapter Summary

A major trend in current college choice research is a focus on the experiences of students from populations traditionally underrepresented in higher education to address issues of access and equity. Falling under the access and equity umbrella, a focus on college preparation was also evident in the review of the last twenty years' literature on college choice. These trends have contributed to the development of college preparation programs and should continue to influence these programs in the future, particularly those intended to increase the higher education participation of students of color and low socioeconomic students.

It is clear from this brief review of college preparation programs that a multifaceted approach to preparing students for college is necessary. Most of the programs discussed here focus on developing the capacity of low socioeconomic students and students of color to engage in behaviors that lead to college enrollment. Foundations, state and local governments, higher education institutions, and the federal government all play a part in ensuring a variety of programs to meet diverse student needs. It is also clear that college preparation extends beyond information and help with completing college applications. Academic preparation, skills development, mentoring, nurturing aspirations, and financial assistance are all essential components of effective college preparation programs. Those that can address most if not all of these components will have the greatest impact on bringing down the many barriers standing in the way of postsecondary education for students of color and low socioeconomic status.

Combining careful program planning to include the essential components outlined by Corwin, Colyar, and Tierney (2005) with a cultural wealth perspective allows those implementing programs to recognize the strengths that students bring with them to the college choice process and to build on those strengths to help students maintain their educational aspirations, plan for their futures, and enact the steps necessary to achieve their educational goals. Asset-oriented lenses assist in preparing students for higher education in ways that honor their cultural backgrounds and values. The next step is to ensure that higher education institutions incorporate these frameworks into their work with students to ensure their success in college. The research points clearly in the direction of supporting the increased diversity in higher education through practices and policies that meet the needs of students from an increasingly wide range of backgrounds. Perhaps in the next twenty years, we will see less stratification in higher education as a result of these efforts.

Implications and Recommendations for Practice, Policy, and Research

THE PRECEDING CHAPTERS REVIEWED the extensive literature related to college choice, focusing on current trends, comprehensive models, and questions about their utility in the current environment, specific experiences of students of color and lower socioeconomic students in the process, and college preparation programs. Framed in the trends of the literature toward focusing on college preparation, movement away from comprehensive models, and policy impacts and implications, all of which further the conversation regarding issues of access and equity, this review of literature illustrates how the field of college choice has advanced in the last twenty years. This chapter outlines the recommendations for practice, policy, and research that emerge from this literature. To illuminate how the field has changed since the publication of Paulsen's monograph (1990), the chapter begins with a summarization of the practice, research, and policy recommendations that emerged from his review of the literature. It then poses a number of recommendations that grow from the more recent literature, thus providing a road map for those who wish to lead the field into the future.

Recommendations for Practice, Policy, and Research from 1989

Paulsen's monograph (1990) was written primarily to enhance the emerging field of enrollment management. The goals of this field, Paulsen argued, were to "plan and forecast their enrollment more effectively" and "to influence the college going decision making process of students more effectively" (p. 71).

The recommendations that flowed from his review of the literature reflect this enrollment-management orientation. Recognizing that enrollment management moved beyond individual institutions, Paulsen incorporated suggestions for research and policy into his monograph as well as recommendations for institutional professionals. Recommendations in each of these areas are briefly described below.

Recommendations for Practice

Paulsen (1990) framed his recommendations for practice as macro- and microlevel. From the macrolevel research that was developed in the 1970s and 1980s, Paulsen observed that institutional enrollment managers could glean information about how environmental factors affected enrollment behaviors. Of particular interest to Paulsen was the impact of economic changes on college enrollment, a factor that is all but invisible in the current research. On the macrolevel, Paulsen recommended that enrollment managers continue to study large-scale data to gain a clearer understanding of how the environment affects enrollment trends.

At the microlevel, Paulsen encouraged professionals to continue to develop an understanding of the effect of student and institutional characteristics and their interactions and to predict and shape enrollment patterns, thus identifying "the student markets with the greatest potential enrollment yield for a particular college or university" (p. 73). Of further interest to professionals, Paulsen suggested, was an increased understanding of college predisposition and the factors that shape it. Noting that predisposition develops early in students' educational careers, Paulsen recommended that professionals look into early intervention as a means for shaping students' eventual postsecondary decisions. When it comes to the search and choice phases of the process, Paulsen argued, institutions should determine which student characteristics are most desirable to them, particularly exploring whether students with those characteristics would benefit from an education at that particular institution. Finally, Paulsen noted, all of these considerations should shape institutional marketing strategies, allowing colleges and universities to capture particular markets of potential students with targeted campaigns.

Although Paulsen acknowledged that some of these processes and interactions might be different for students from different cultural backgrounds, none of his recommendations for practice reflect current trends toward addressing the stratification of higher education: it is a clear, new direction in the last twenty years. Brief recommendations for research and policy follow.

Recommendations for Research and Policy

It is important to note that Paulsen's recommendations for research and policy are directed primarily at institutional agents and incorporate an umbrella suggestion for the increased development of databases institutions can use to engage in the recommendations for practice listed above. For example, Paulsen recommended that research focus on what he called "nontraditional" students. Nontraditional for Paulsen included students of color, women, international students, graduate students, and adult students. Understanding the perceptions of students from these groups, Paulsen suggested, would allow institutions to better serve their educational needs. Although the field has clearly responded to the call for increased understanding of the college choice experiences of students of color, research involving adult students, graduate students, and international students is still sparse.

The search process was the focus of another of Paulsen's recommendations. This information could be used to better understand the timing and sequences (p. 79) of students' institutional choices. Again the focus of this recommendation is on increasing an institution's ability to market its programs effectively to potential students and not on the idea of increasing access to higher education for underrepresented students that is prevalent in the more current research and recommendations. To aid in the development of effective marketing strategies, Paulsen also recommended the development of databases providing information on the interactions among institutional, student, and environmental characteristics. Perhaps this focus on quantitative research has influenced the large number of quantitative studies in the current research. The prevalence of studies based on large-scale longitudinal quantitative studies certainly answered Paulsen's call; however, qualitative research may be better situated to understand the nuances in the experiences of today's diverse college-going population.

Finally, Paulsen called for increased state and federal involvement in both the generation of college choice research and the development of policies that support this research. Such research, he argued, could lead to increased incentives for taxpayers' support for programs such as financial aid that are intended to increase access to higher education. In essence, Paulsen's argument was that the more we know about enrollment behaviors, the more effectively we can direct resources and policies to encourage college enrollment.

Clearly the college choice arena has taken on a new focus in the last twenty years. This shift could be described as moving from developing an understanding of the students who are enrolling in higher education to endeavoring to make higher education an option that is accessible to those students as well as those who otherwise might not choose to enroll in college. This shift is evident not only in the research generated in the last twenty years but also as a primary focus of the practice, policy, and research recommendations that emerge from that research.

Recommendations for Practice, Policy, and Research from the Current Research

Many recommendations from the current research are based on the idea that continued effort is necessary to resolve issues of access to higher education for low socioeconomic students and students of color. This emphasis reflects the general trend away from comprehensive models of college choice and shifting attention toward specific groups of students who have traditionally been underserved in the higher education arena. These recommendations are presented here to act as a guide for future conversations, policy forums, research endeavors, professionals, and researchers interested in increasing broader access to higher education.

Recommendations for Practice

For the purpose of outlining this group of recommendations, "practice" is defined as programs and behaviors that can be implemented from individual to midinstitutional levels. The impact might be felt by groups of students or by individuals. What is essential is not the scope of the program but its ability to make a difference, particularly at the level of face-to-face interaction with students. A significant element of success at this level of recommendations is a paradigm shift that may need to occur at the individual level. If individuals make assumptions about students based on the groups to which they belong and act on those assumptions, the ability to assist students in accessing institutions that may seem unwelcoming is diminished. Changing how students interface with institutional agents takes more than a flashy program; attitudes and beliefs about both individuals and groups must change to effectively implement these programs. Recommendations for practice fall into three broad categories: changes in practice that involve paradigm shifts for individuals, changes that relate to college preparation programs, and recommendations for institutions.

Individual Paradigm Shifts. Cultural wealth and cultural relevance drive recommendations that focus on individual paradigm shifts to affect practice. For example, Freeman (1997), Knight, Norton, Bentley, and Dixon (2004), and Tierney (2002) recommended that high school and college personnel interact with students in culturally relevant ways. These researchers emphasized the ability to understand students' contexts as an essential factor when providing advice and information. Cultural relevance also has a place in the curriculum, allowing students to bring their whole selves to the classroom and relate the curriculum to their life experience.

Moving teachers, counselors, college representatives, and other personnel who hold biases based on group stereotypes to a perspective that views students through an asset-oriented lens (Garcia and Guerra, 2004) requires a paradigm shift that is difficult for many. Programs and schools desiring to assist students from a variety of backgrounds in successfully navigating the college choice process must commit time and resources to developing culturally relevant processes and ingraining them in individual practice.

College Preparation Programs. Recommendations for practice related to college preparation programs also focus on cultural relevance. For example, Perez and McDonough (2008) suggested that an "individualistic approach" (p. 261) to educating Latina and Latino students and their families about higher education will not work. Rather, programs interested in increasing the participation of Latinas and Latinos in higher education must incorporate layers of community, family, and friendship groups, tapping into all network resources that Latina and Latino students use in the college choice process. Solorzano (1992) and Perna and Titus (2005) also focused on family involvement as a type of cultural relevance essential to the college preparation of students of color. Using the Puente program as a model, Tierney (2002) suggested that involving parents in college preparation programs not only builds encouragement of their children's educational plans but also helps parents understand the need to let their students go (p. 601) and feel good about their foray into the higher education environment. All these authors argued that college preparation programs need to consider students' context to effectively assist them in the college choice process, noting that possession of various forms of capital can be viewed as assets rather than deficits.

Challenges to this approach lie in the nature of college preparation programs. For the sake of efficiency, programs may push students through particular steps and processes that do not take into consideration their individual contexts. Doing so may result in some students feeling disconnected from the very processes intended to encourage their participation in higher education. Careful planning for meeting individual students' needs in college preparation programs is necessary for their effectiveness, and the cultural wealth paradigm (Villalpando and Solorzano, 2005) provides an excellent frame for these efforts.

Institutional Recommendations. Also grounded in cultural relevancy are school and college recommendations. For example, addressing the growing privatization of college guidance counseling for high school students, McDonough, Korn, and Yamasaki (1997) suggested that both the high school counseling and college admissions fields must enter into dialogue to determine who will take responsibility for assisting students in the transition from high school to college (p. 316). College and high school personnel need to revisit the issue of guidance counseling to ensure that students who most need postsecondary information can get it.

Other researchers (Cabrera and LaNasa, 2001; Mullen, 2009; Smith, 2007) suggested that higher education institutions are largely responsible for making information available. Mullen and Smith noted that this approach is particularly important for selective institutions interested in increasing the participation of underserved student populations, while Cabrera and LaNasa lauded the potential role of admissions officers in helping parents make connections between higher education and economic benefits, providing information on financial planning, making available adequate information about financial aid availability and applications, and explaining the role of curricular planning in preparing for college (p. 142). These strategies increase the social and cultural capital parents provide for their children during the college choice process. Mullen and Smith focused on elite institutions that have the resources to provide high-achieving low socioeconomic students with information necessary to apply and enroll. Less selective institutions that do not have the same resources available for targeted outreach, however, will have to weigh their commitment to increasing access for underrepresented students against budgetary constraints.

Gonzales, Stoner, and Jovel (2003) focused their recommendations on high schools, arguing that to provide access to the higher levels of capital necessary to actualize these students' educational aspirations, high school personnel must understand the implications of their "institutional abuse or neglect" (p. 167), which for the Latina students in their study was limited postsecondary opportunities. For K–12, Gutman and McLoyd (2000) offered recommendations that included assisting parents in helping their children with schoolwork, greater teacher involvement with parents, and the organization of educational programming for both higher- and lower-achieving students to increase families' access to information about educational opportunities. Mentoring was also explored (Hamrick and Stage, 2004), and the role of the principal was emphasized as important to setting the organizational climate around the support of students of color and lower socioeconomic students (Muhammad, 2008; Solorzano and Ornelas, 2004).

Educational aspirations are a necessary but not sufficient condition for students' enrollment in college. If barriers for colleges, schools, or classrooms or in individual interactions are removed, students of color and lower socioeconomic students have a greater chance of actualizing their aspirations. These recommendations for practice all focus on removing those barriers. Most of these practice-oriented recommendations affect individuals or small groups of students as they interact with institutional agents for both high school and higher education. Barriers also exist in policy. The recommendations for policy discussed in the next section have the potential for a broader impact on removing those barriers at the institutional, state, and federal levels.

Recommendations for Policy

Although implications for practice have the potential to effect change for individual students in specific institutional contexts, recommendations for policy are typically intended to have a larger institutional or systemic impact. The suggestions for policy in the research on college choice are no exception. Generally, the recommendations presented below fall into four broad categories: school policy, K–16 alliances, financial aid policy, and general suggestions for guiding policy exploration. In each area, the policies are primarily focused on addressing issues of access and equity in higher education, with a clear goal of increasing the college enrollment of students from populations traditionally underrepresented in higher education.

School Policy. Several recommendations focused on the development of policies that support college preparation for K–12 students. Cabrera and LaNasa's study (2001) showed that college qualification is a key element of college enrollment, particularly for disadvantaged youth, who rely on the social and cultural capital provided by college preparation courses to increase their likelihood of college enrollment. Essential to policies in this area is the understanding that getting on the college preparation track occurs as early as late grade school, so sixth, seventh, and eighth graders must have a clear idea of which courses lead toward college to stay on track for college qualification. Related to the idea of college qualification, Gonzales, Stoner, and Jovel (2003) recommended the formation of policies that examine the processes by which students of color are placed in special education and English as a Second Language programs, which "[prevent] and [delay] access to any kind of college preparation curriculum" (p. 167). Often such policies are developed by states or districts, so large-scale policy shifts are necessary to address identified inequities.

K–16 Alliances. Several authors recommended the formation of alliances between higher education institutions and K–12 schools (Cabrera and LaNasa, 2001; Hurtado, Inkelas, Briggs, and Rhee, 1997; Pitre, 2006a). These partnerships require the cooperation and coordination of both K–12 and higher education institutions. Cabrera and LaNasa posited that such partnerships could begin as early as elementary school and suggested that parents' involvement is a key element of such partnerships. Pitre's focus was on smoothing transitions throughout a student's educational process—from elementary to middle school, from middle school to high school, and from high school to college. Hurtado, Inkelas, Briggs, and Rhee joined Pitre in arguing that both K–12 schools and higher education institutions are responsible for preparing students to make college enrollment decisions.

Perna and Titus (2004) focused on state policies, recommending that states consider a K–16 approach. Echoing Cabrera and LaNasa's recommendation for educational partnerships, these authors urged state policymakers to consider ways to make the pathway to college more fluid. In particular, the authors noted that high school enrollment patterns, including the curricula students engage in high school, affects college enrollment. As shapers of student's K–12 enrollment patterns, K–12 personnel must understand what is required for college qualification and ensure that students with the ability or desire to enroll in postsecondary education are making adequate progress toward qualification.

Financial Aid Policy. The availability of financial aid was shown in the literature to affect students of color and lower socioeconomic status about whether and where to attend college. Perna (2000) and Paulsen and St. John (2002) argued that the current financial aid environment does not benefit students of color and low-income students. The high tuition–high aid paradigm that has dominated financial aid policy for the last twenty years, along with an increasing dependence on loans, has made financing a college education very difficult for students who are located in lower income brackets. These authors recommend that national policymakers attend to this finding in discussions about the future of federal financial aid programs. Perna, Steele, Woda, and Hibbert (2005) reiterated the importance of state aid policies in increasing access to higher education for students of color. Policies directed at increasing the educational aspirations of students will fall flat if students of color and lower socioeconomic status cannot afford the educations they desire.

Also related to financial aid, Perna and Titus (2004) recommended several changes with an emphasis on state policymakers. First, they argued that one way to promote enrollment in a state's public institutions is to keep tuition low at those institutions. Berger and Kostal (2002) also supported a low-tuition approach to increasing college participation through appropriations to higher education systems and the distribution of student tuition aid. Second, Perna and Titus noted that need-based aid paid directly to students from both the state and institutions can increase college choices across types of institutions. This type of aid is particularly effective at reducing the public-private (p. 520) tuition gap and allowing more students access to private institutions. Many states suffer from a brain drain, in which the best and brightest high school graduates leave the state to attend college. Perna and Titus suggested that increased state appropriations to higher education could help reduce brain drain.

Focusing on federal policy, Lillis (2008) suggested that the current high tuition–high aid higher education environment be reevaluated. He noted that "current policies fail to accurately identify or satisfactorily meet the current needs of potential college-bound students" (pp. 28–29). Citing the trend of increased class stratification in the private college sector, Lillis urged federal policymakers to revisit the shift in federal aid from grants to loans, which he argued does not serve lower-income students who have limited access to economic capital.

Exploration of Future Policy. The final group of policy recommendations is broader and develops questions for policymakers to consider. For example, McDonough, Antonio, and Trent's and Freeman's policy considerations (1997) included examining ways to engage African American students in the college choice process even if their parents were not active in this process; addressing the roles that K–12 and higher education institutions play in encouraging African American students' educational attainment, particularly as related to cultural concerns and the barriers they perceive as they consider their educational options; exploring how African Americans access information, specifically regarding labor market benefits of a higher education; and examining geographic trends of students staying closer to home to focus recruitment strategies on untapped local populations like adult students of other races.

Other researchers focused on state policies. For example, Perna and Titus (2004) recommended attention to the composition of a state's higher education system, which affects students' habitus for enrollment. Students, they argued, have more information about institutions closer to home. As they collect and consider this information, their ideas about what college is like are shaped by the composition of local institutions. This information becomes what is familiar or comfortable to them, and it shapes the choices that fit their habitus. State policies should consider both the range of institutions offered as well as how they provide resources for marketing those institutions.

Although McDonough, Ventresca, and Outcalt (2000) did not directly recommend policy, the concerns they express about the growing privatization of the college guidance and counseling process are appropriate for consideration by state policymakers. These authors argued that schools have essentially given responsibility for gathering postsecondary information to students, resulting in an information gap between students from different socioeconomic backgrounds, as those who have more economic capital have access to more information. McDonough and her colleagues asserted that because higher education has a public benefit, the public has an interest in ensuring access to a broad range of students, which is not met by the trend toward privatization. Because school structures are dictated by state and district policies, the implicit implication in McDonough, Ventresca, and Outcalt's argument is that this issue should be addressed through policy.

For federal policymakers, Karen's study (2002) of changes in access to higher education from 1980 to 1992 led him to suggest that creating a diverse student population in American higher education will require continued, if not broader, policies related to affirmative action for students of color, women, and low socioeconomic status. He found that students from social backgrounds that provide capital not necessarily valued in higher education continue to lag behind in their participation in postsecondary education. Similarly, Teranishi, Allen, and Solorzano (2004) argued that changes in policy related to college choice must begin by examining "racial segregation and inequities in educational resources and postsecondary preparation" (p. 2243). Further, they noted, in light of the increasing diversity across the United States, policies must address schools' attention to traditional practices that were developed for middle-class white populations. Karen and Teranishi, Allen, and Solorzano focused on broader social issues that affect policies intended to increase access to higher education for students of color and lower socioeconomic status.

Institutional, state, and federal policies are all driven to some extent by research related to the issues of interest to policymakers. In the area of college choice and in particular those studies examining issues of access and equity in this process, additional research is needed to guide future policy decisions. A number of studies cited above provided suggestions for the direction of future research, many of which focus on generating a better understanding of the college choice process for students of color and low socioeconomic status. For example, McDonough, Korn, and Yamasaki (1997) suggested that scholars interested in improving access to higher education should continue to ask questions about how first-generation and low-income students as well as students of color access the assistance they need to complete the college choice and enrollment process.

Recommendations for Future Research

Ideally policy is guided by research. Much of the current research provides directions for future research related to increasing the postsecondary participation of students of color and low socioeconomic status. Many recommendations call for continued attention to differences in the process by race, ethnicity, and social class. Others focus on a further examination of high school context and factors that play into the gap between aspirations and achievement. This section includes several recommendations for research based on the changing landscape of higher education.

Race, Ethnicity, Social Class, and the College Choice Process. A number of research recommendations urge researchers to examine differences in the college choice process for different groups of students. Related is McDonough, Antonio, and Horvat's suggestion (1996) that future research "identify how different forms of capital and different investment strategies and goals could be used to predict choice of college" (p. 22). Perna (2000) also recommended exploration of institutional choice, noting that future research should focus on the processes used by students from different racial and ethnic backgrounds to select a two-year college. These recommendations move the focus away from different types of students to how capital affects the type of institution students select. Even shifting away from the student, however, the thrust of this research direction is to consider ways to equalize access to a wide variety of institutions for an increasingly diverse college-going population.

Addtionally, Delgado-Gaitan (1992) called for research exploring "family learning environments" (p. 513) to help educators better understand how to support students from different racial and ethnic groups in their educational endeavors. Kao and Thompson (2003) recommended that research look into the advantages of group membership for students from immigrant and families of color, embracing the cultural wealth perspective. Such a focus, the authors suggested, can assist educators in changing their own perspectives of students from these populations. Freeman (1999) noted that African American students' experiences are distinctive and should be studied in the future as such. Hamrick and Stage (2004) found that the predisposition variables in their study had different predictive significance by racial and ethnic group and urged future researchers to explore those differences. Teranishi and others (2004) took this argument a level deeper, calling for research that examines variations in experience for students from different ethnic groups in the Asian Pacific American population. It is clear from this strand of studies that research should continue to delve into the nuanced experiences of students of color to inform the policy recommendations outlined above.

Perna (2000) also recommended that research inquire into how students from different racial and ethnic backgrounds develop expectations regarding the returns on an educational investment. Her study suggested that African American students expect fewer benefits from earning a college degree than white and Hispanic students, which may account for their lower enrollment in higher education. Perna argued that this potential cause of the stratification of higher education in the United States warrants further exploration.

High School Context. Another group of studies recommended further exploration into the impact of school segregation on educational aspirations, achievement, and attainment (Perna, 2000; Perna and Titus, 2005; Solorzano, 1992; Teranishi, Allen, and Solorzano, 2004). Mixed findings regarding the role of schools with high numbers of students of color are behind this research emphasis. For example, Perna's study found that segregated schools increased the likelihood of college enrollment for African Americans, while Perna and Titus's research found that segregated high schools decreased the probability of college enrollment for Hispanic students. Solorzano (1992) and Teranishi, Allen, and Solorzano (2004) called for a closer examination of how resources are distributed to highly segregated schools, noting that limited resources have a negative impact on college preparation and enrollment for students of color in these schools. Understanding the role of school segregation can also drive state and district policy to produce more equitable outcomes for students of color.

One concern of researchers who urged further exploration into the gap between aspirations and achievement is the role of schools (Hamrick and Stage, 2004). Kao and Tienda (1998) echoed Hamrick and Stage's call for research exploring the disconnect between aspirations and attainment for students of color. Both sets of authors were troubled by the fact that educational aspirations of students of color are higher than those of white students, while their college participation is significantly lower. Further, both sets of authors suggested that future research should inform the creation of programs and policies intended to help students maintain high aspirations throughout their high school years and to engage in behaviors that lead to the fulfillment of those aspirations.

Other Future Directions. The recommendations that emerged from the research reviewed for this monograph clearly reflect the trends in the field away from comprehensive models and toward better understandings of college preparation and policy implications that feed our understanding of access and equity issues in higher education. The changing landscape of higher education, however, demands that we continue to broaden our research horizons, addressing issues for other groups of students entering the postsecondary arena. For example, research on the college choice process of adult students, one of the fastest-growing student populations, is lacking. Echoing Paulsen's call (1990) for a better understanding of these students, research exploring the experiences of adult students should be added to the higher education agenda. Another student population whose college choice experiences are invisible in the current research is the lesbian, gay, bisexual, and transgendered population. These students make choices in the context of their sexual identity, similar to the ways that students of color and lower socioeconomic status must navigate the choice process through their social identities. A better understanding of these choices would lead to improved services for them. Additionally, given the U.S. involvement in military conflicts in the Middle East in the last several years, research examining how students navigate the nuances of military alternatives and opportunities (such as the GI bill and ROTC) will enhance our ability to ensure access to higher education institutions for students who have served or are serving in the military. Finally, with the growth of for-profit and distance education, future research might consider the college choice processes of students who select these options.

Together, these recommendations for practice, policy, and future research guide the future of the college choice field. Evident in all three is the call for increased attention to the specific experiences of groups with different social identities as they move through the college choice process. Additionally, all three represent a movement away from looking at how to "fix" students and their families to seeking solutions for the stratification of higher education in educational systems, social contexts, and policies. This movement reflects a cultural wealth paradigm, enhancing the ability to identify and address the barriers diverse groups of students face as they decide whether and where to go to college.

Conclusion

A vast body of research on college choice has emerged in the past twenty years. Clearly, the emphasis in the college choice field has moved away from the focus on enrollment management predominant in Paulsen's monograph (1990). Armed with models that allowed for the explication of variables significant to the process, researchers have conducted hundreds of studies designed to clarify how students determine whether and where to go to college. Given this factor, what do we know about college choice? And where is the field headed from here?

What We Know

The studies analyzed in this monograph provide clear answers to these questions. First and foremost is the clear trend toward addressing issues of access and equity in the choice process. Stratification of higher education institutions by race, ethnicity, and social class continues to prohibit the achievement of lofty goals of educating the whole society in the nation's colleges and universities. Moving away from simply trying to understand the enrollment behaviors of students who choose to go to college, the field is almost singularly focused on addressing the factors that contribute to the decisions of many students—primarily students of color and lower socioeconomic status—not to attend college.

Second, we know that students move through stages as they consider whether and where to go to college. We also know, however, that these stages are neither linear nor uniform for all students. Many students simply *know* they will go to college after high school, while for others the decision is one that leads to anxiety, confusion, and extensive planning. Students for whom attending college is a step out of their habitus experience predisposition, search, and choice differently from those who feel this expectation from the beginning of their conscious thinking about education. We know then that comprehensive models, while useful for generating a broad understanding of the college choice process, do not meet the needs of practitioners, policymakers, and researchers interested in increasing the participation of underrepresented students in higher education. The recommendations for practice, policy, and research clearly indicate that we need more information about the nuances of the process for these vastly different students. Newer models have entered the field, focusing on how context plays into students' enrollment decisions and expanding the concept of rational choice in ways not considered before. These models offer new explanations and recommendations for policy, practice, and research as they are refined and tested in the future.

Third, we know that students are not being equitably prepared for college. Segregation in K–12 schools by race, ethnicity, and social class inhibits students' learning. Students of color and lower socioeconomic status are disproportionately represented in low-resource schools and tend to rely more on their schools for information when their families are not able to provide it. Yet because of a lack of resources, these students are often denied the assistance of a college-going school culture and school personnel who can provide culturally relevant, adequate information. Additionally, tracking continues to lower the academic preparation of students of color and lower socioeconomic status. In an environment where we know that a rigorous high school curriculum enhances students' chances of success in higher education, students of color and lower socioeconomic status have less access to Advanced Placement courses than white middle- and upper-class students. All these factors result in less preparation for college, which discourages students from enrolling in college and contributes to the continued stratification of higher education.

Finally, an increased focus on policy implications and recommendations is also characteristic of the last twenty years of college choice research. Although Paulsen's recommendations (1990) were largely focused on institutional agents, current recommendations range from individual to institutional, state, and national policies. And they cross from individual impact to group impact to broader societal impact. Of primary importance in policy recommendations is an awareness of how the federal financial aid environment affects access to higher education. The research into current financial aid policy is clear: without availability of a variety of financial aid opportunities, including grants and need-based scholarships, students with limited financial resources cannot enact the process of choosing whether and where to go to college in the same ways that their middle- and upper-class peers do. The assumption is clear: policy shapes the future of higher education in many ways, and effective policies are essential to adequately address issues of access and equity.

Where We Are Going

In addition to these trends across the literature, new lenses shape the way we think about and examine college choice. Knowing more about specific students' experiences of the college choice process requires shifts in the way we conceptualize students. The cultural wealth perspective provides a new lens for viewing students who have previously been seen as problems that need fixing. Incorporating this perspective in their research has allowed many authors whose work is described in these chapters to see more clearly the barriers that impede the educational attainment of students of color and low socioeconomic status. Seeing these barriers with fresh eyes means moving away from blaming groups for their lower participation rates in higher education and recognizing the impact of educational systems that do not meet certain groups' needs, social contexts, and policies intended to help these groups that actually serve to reinforce the barriers to their participation. The research in this monograph begins to identify problematic factors external to the individuals experiencing the college choice process and urges attention to them. A continued emphasis on addressing these barriers is an important next step for practitioners, policymakers, and researchers interested in reducing the stratification that persists in higher education. Essential to this step is a continued effort to incorporate the cultural wealth perspective into all our efforts.

Although we have a reasonably clear picture of the variables that affect students' experiences with the college choice process, we know less about how these variables interact. For example, we know that individual and institutional characteristics play into students' enrollment decisions, but we do not understand how they play against and with each other to create a sense of fit for individual students. Additionally, we know the kinds of factors that influence predisposition, but we still do not know how students' understandings of education are formed through the interaction of family background, school context, and academic performance. The vast majority of current college choice research consists of quantitative studies using large preexisting databases analyzed post hoc by researchers attempting to identify and further explicate significant variables. What is needed to move the field forward in its understanding of the nuances of the process are carefully planned and executed qualitative and mixed-method studies that can delve into the how and why questions that blur our clear understanding of how students experience the process of making postsecondary education decisions. Collaborative projects that involve students from a variety of backgrounds allow for the disaggregation of racial and ethnic groups that is also needed.

The field of college choice is on the cusp of taking a leap forward. Building on the strong efforts of research from the last twenty years, practitioners, policymakers, and researchers can move the field forward in ways that will begin to address the inequities that have plagued higher education for decades. The recommendations provided throughout this monograph provide a road map for those interested in embracing the challenge of taking the field of college choice headlong into the twenty-first century.

References

Adelman, C. (2006). *The toolbox revisited: Paths to degree completion from high school through college*. Washington, DC: United States Department of Education.

Alwin, D. F., and Otto, L. B. (1977). High school context effects on aspirations. *Sociology of Education, 50*(4), 259–273.

Attinasi, L. C., Jr. (1989). Getting in: Mexican Americans' perceptions of university attendance and the implications for freshman year persistence. *Journal of Higher Education, 60*(3), 247–277.

Avery, C., and Hoxby, C. M. (2004). Do and should financial aid packages affect students' college choices? In C. M. Hoxby (Ed.), *College choices: The economics of where to go, when to go, and how to pay for it* (pp. 239–302). Chicago: University of Chicago Press.

Azmitia, M., and Cooper, C. R. (2001). Good or bad? Peer influences on Latino and European American adolescents' pathways through school. *Journal of Education for Students Placed at Risk, 6*(1–2), 45–71.

Beattie, I. R. (2002). Are all "adolescent econometricians" created equal? Racial, class, and gender differences in college enrollment. *Sociology of Education, 75*(1), 19–43.

Berger, M. C., and Kostal, T. (2002). Financial resources, regulation, and enrollment in U.S. public higher education. *Economics of Education Review, 21*, 101–110.

Bergerson, A. A. (2007). Exploring the impact of social class on adjustment to college: Anna's story. *International Journal of Qualitative Studies in Education, 20*(1), 99–119.

Bergerson, A. A., Heiselt, A., Aiken-Wisniewski, S., and Thompson, S. (2005, November). *A second look at the college choice process: Reflections of women on their postsecondary education choices.* Paper presented at the annual meeting of the Association for the Study of Higher Education, Philadelphia, PA.

Bers, T. H., and Galowich, P. M. (2002). Using survey and focus group research to learn about parents' role in the community college choice process. *Community College Review, 29*(4), 67–83.

Bloom, J. (2007). (Mis)reading social class in the journey towards college: Youth development in urban America. *Teachers College Record, 109*(2), 343–368.

Borus, M. E., and Carpenter, S. A. (1984). Factors associated with college attendance of high school seniors. *Economics of Education Review 3*(3), 169–176.

Bourdieu, P. (1977). Cultural reproduction and social reproduction. In J. Karabel and A. H. Halsey (Eds.). *Power and ideology in education* (pp. 487–511). New York: Oxford University.

Bourdieu, P. (1987/[1979]). The forms of capital. In J. G. Richardson (Ed.), *Handbook of theory and research for the sociology of education*. New York: Greenwood Press.

Bourdieu, P. (1993). *The field of cultural production.* New York: Columbia University Press.

Bourdieu, P., and Wacquant, L.J.D. (1992). *An invitation to reflexive sociology.* Chicago: University of Chicago Press.

Bouse, G. A., and Hossler, D. (1991). Studying college choice: A progress report. *Journal of College Admission, 130*, 11–16.

Breen, R., and Goldthorpe, J. H. (1997). Explaining educational differentials: Towards a formal rational action theory. *Rationality and Society, 9*(3), 275–305.

Brooks, R. (2003). Young people's higher education choices: The role of family and friends. *British Journal of Sociology of Education, 24*(3), 283–297.

Cabrera, A. F., and others. (2006). Increasing the college preparedness of at-risk students. *Journal of Latinos and Education, 5*(2), 79–97.

Cabrera, A. F., and LaNasa, S. M. (2000). Understanding the college-choice process. *New Directions for Institutional Research, 107*, 5–22.

Cabrera, A. F., and LaNasa, S. M. (2001). On the path to college: Three critical tasks facing America's disadvantaged. *Research in Higher Education, 42*(2), 119–149.

Callendar, D., and Jackson, J. (2008). Does the fear of debt constrain choice of university or subject of study? *Studies in Higher Education, 33*(4), 405–429.

Chapman, D. W. (1981). A model of student college choice. *Journal of Higher Education, 52*(5), 490–505.

Chapman, R., and Jackson, R. (1987). *College choices of academically able students.* New York: College Entrance Examination Board.

Conley, D. (2001). Parental assets and postsecondary schooling. *Sociology of Education, 74*(1), 59–72.

Cooper, C. R., and others. (1995). Bridging students' multiple worlds: African American and Latino youth in academic outreach programs. In R. F. Macias and R. G. Garcia Ramos (Eds.), *Changing schools for changing students: An anthology of research on language minorities* (pp. 211–234). Santa Barbara: University of California Linguistic Minority Research Institute.

Corwin, Z. B., Colyar, J. E., and Tierney, W. G. (2005). Introduction. Engaging research and practice: Extracurricular and curricular influences on college access. In W. G. Tierney, Z. B. Corwin, and J. E. Colyar (Eds.), *Preparing for college: Nine elements of effective outreach* (pp. 1–9). Albany, NY: SUNY Press.

Curs, B., and Singell, L. D., Jr. (2002). An analysis of the application and enrollment processes for in-state and out-of-state students at a large public university. *Economics of Education Review, 21*, 111–124.

Davis–Van Atta, D. L., and Carrier, S. C. (1986). Using the institutional research office. In D. Hossler (Ed.), *Managing college enrollments.* New Directions for Higher Education, no. 53. San Francisco: Jossey-Bass.

Delgado-Gaitan, C. (1992). School matters in the Mexican American home: Socializing children to education. *American Educational Research Journal, 29*(3), 495–513.

DesJardins, S. L., Ahlburg, D. A., and McCall, B. P. (2006). An integrated model of application, admission, enrollment, and financial aid. *Journal of Higher Education, 77*(3), 381–429.

DesJardins, S. L., Dundar, H., and Hendel, D. D. (1999). Modeling the college application decision process in a land-grant university. *Economics of Education Review, 18*, 117–132.

Dixon, P. N., and Martin, N. K. (1991). Measuring factors that influence college choice. *NASPA Journal, 29*(1), 31–36.

Dynarski, S. (2002). The behavioral and distributional implications of aid for college. *American Economic Review, 92*(2), 279–285.

Dynarski, S. (2003). Does aid matter? Measuring the effect of student aid on college attendance and completion. *American Economic Review, 93*(1), 279–288.

Ellwood, D. T., and Kane, T. J. (2000). Who is getting a college education? Family background and growing gaps in enrollment. In S. Danziger and J. Waldfogel (Eds.), *Securing the future: Investing in children from birth to college* (pp. 283–324). New York: Russell Sage Foundation.

Fashola, O. S., and Slavin, R. E. (1997, February). Effective dropout prevention and college attendance programs for Latino students. Paper presented at the annual meeting of the American Educational Research Association, Chicago, IL.

Fenske, R. H., Geranios, C. A., Keller, J. E., and Moore, D. E. (1997). *Early intervention programs: Opening the door to higher education.* ASHE-ERIC Higher Education Report, Vol. 25, No. 6. Washington, DC: ERIC Clearinghouse on Higher Education.

Flint, T. A. (1997). Intergenerational effects of paying for college. *Research in Higher Education, 38*(3), 313–344.

Freeman, K. (1997). Increasing African Americans' participation in higher education: African American high school students' perspectives. *Journal of Higher Education, 68*(5), 523–550.

Freeman, K. (1999). The race factor in African Americans' college choice. *Urban Education, 34*(1), 4–25.

Galotti, K.K.M., and Mark, M. C. (1994). How do high school students structure an important life decision? A short-term longitudinal study of the college decision-making process. *Research in Higher Education, 35*(5), 589–607.

Gandara, P. (1999). Telling stories of success: Cultural capital and the educational mobility of Chicano students. *Latino Studies Journal, 10*(1), 38–51.

Gandara, P. (2002). A study of high school Puente: What we have learned about preparing Latino youth for postsecondary education. *Educational Policy, 16*(4), 474–495.

Garcia, S. B., and Guerra, P. L. (2004). Deconstructing deficit thinking: Working with educators to create more equitable learning environments. *Education and Urban Society, 36(2)*, 150–168.

Gardner, P. W., Ritblatt, W. N., and Beatty, J. R. (2000). Academic achievement and parental school involvement as a function of high school size. *High School Journal, 83*(2), 21–27.

Gibson, M. A., Gandara, P., and Koyama, J. P. (2004). The role of peers in the schooling of U.S. Mexican youth. In M. Gibson, P. Gandara, and J. P. Koyama (Eds.), *School connections: U.S. Mexican youth, peers, and school achievement* (pp. 1–17). New York: Teachers College Press.

Gladieux, L. E. (2004). Low-income students and the affordability of higher education. In R. D. Kahlenberg (Ed.), *America's untapped resource: Low-income students in higher education* (pp. 17–57). New York: Century Foundation Press.

Goddard, R. D. (2003). Relational networks, social trust, and norms: A social capital perspective on students' chances of academic success. *Educational Evaluation and Policy Analysis, 25*(1), 59–74.

Goenner, C. F., and Pauls, K. (2006). A predictive model of inquiry to enrollment. *Research in Higher Education, 47*(1), 935–956.

Gonzales, K. P., Stoner, C., and Jovel, J. E. (2003). Examining the role of social capital in access to college for Latinas: Toward a college opportunity framework. *Journal of Hispanic Higher Education, 2*(1), 146–170.

Grodsky, E. (2002). Constrained opportunity and student choice in American higher education. *Dissertation Abstracts International, 63*(8), 3008-A.

Grodsky, E., and Jones, T. M. (2007). Real and imagined barriers to college entry: Perceptions of cost. *Social Science Research, 36*, 745–766.

Grubb, W. N., Lara, C. M., and Valdez, S. (2002). Counselor, coordinator, monitor, mom: The roles of counselors in the Puente program. *Educational Policy, 16*(4), 547–571.

Gutman, L. M, and McLoyd, V. C. (2000). Parents' management of their children's education within the home, at school, and in the community: An examination of African American families living in poverty. *Urban Review, 32*(1), 1–24.

Hallinan, M. T. (2000). On the linkages between sociology and race and ethnicity and sociology of education. In M. T. Hallinan (Ed.), *Handbook of the sociology of education* (pp. 65–84). New York: Kluwer Academic/Plenum.

Hamrick, F. A., and Hossler, D. (1996). Diverse information-gathering methods in postsecondary decision-making process. *Review of Higher Education, 19*(2), 179–198.

Hamrick, F. A., and Stage, F. K. (1995, November). Student predisposition to college in high minority enrollment, high school lunch participation schools. Paper presented at the annual meeting of the Association for the Study of Higher Education, Orlando, FL.

Hamrick, F. A., and Stage, F. K. (2000). Community activities, educational mentors, and college predisposition decisions of white, African American, and Hispanic eighth graders. Paper presented at the annual meeting of the American Educational Research Association, New Orleans, LA.

Hamrick, F. A., and Stage, F. K. (2004). College predisposition at high-minority enrollment, low-income schools. *Review of Higher Education, 27*(2), 151–168.

Hanson, S. L. (1994). Unrealized educational aspirations and expectations among U.S. youths. *Sociology of Education, 67*(3), 159–183.

Hao, L., and Bonstead-Bruns, M. (1998). Parent–child differences in educational expectations and the academic achievement of immigrant and native students. *Sociology of Education, 71*(3), 175–198.

Hartley, M., and Morphew, C. C. (2008). What's being sold and to what end? A content analysis of college workbooks. *Journal of Higher Education, 79*(6), 671–691.

Hatcher, R. (1998). Class differentiation in education: Rational choices? *British Journal of Sociology of Education, 19*(1), 5–24.

Hauser, R. M., and Anderson, D. K. (1991). Post–high school plans and aspirations of black and white high school seniors: 1976–1986. *Sociology of Education, 64*(4), 263–277.

Hearn, J. C. (1984). The relative roles of academic, ascribed, and socioeconomic characteristics in college destination. *Sociology of Education, 57*(1), 22–30.

Hearn, J. C. (1991). Academic and nonacademic influences on the college destinations of 1980 high school graduates. *Sociology of Education, 64*(3), 158–171.

Heller, D. E. (1997). Student price response in higher education: An update to Leslie and Brinkman. *Journal of Higher Education, 68*(6), 624–659.

Heller, D. E. (1999). The effects of tuition and state financial aid on public college enrollment. *Review of Higher Education, 21*(1), 65–89.

Henrickson, L. (2002). Old wine in a new wineskin: College choice, college access using agent-based modeling. *Social Sciences Computer Review, 20*(4), 400–419.

Hensley, L. G., and Kinser, K. (2001). Rethinking adult learner persistence: Implications for counselors. *Adultspan Journal, 3*(2), 88–100.

Hofferth, S. L., Boisjoly, J., and Duncan, G. T. (1998). Parents' extrafamilial resources and children's school attainment. *Sociology of Education, 71*(3), 246–268.

Horn, L. J. (1997). *Confronting the odds: Students at risk and the pipeline to higher education.* NCES-98-094. Washington, DC: U.S. Department of Education.

Horvat, E. M. (2001). Understanding equity and access in higher education: The potential contribution of Pierre Bourdieu. In J.C. Smart and W.G. Tierney (Eds.), *Higher education: Handbook of theory and research* (Vol. 16, pp. 195–238). New York: Agathon.

Horvat, E. M., and Antonio, A. L. (1999). "Hey, those shoes are out of uniform": African American girls in an elite high school and the importance of habitus. *Anthropology & Education Quarterly, 30*(3), 317–342.

Hossler, D. (2000). The role of financial aid in enrollment management. *New Directions for Student Services, 89*, 77–90.

Hossler, D., Braxton, J., and Coopersmith, G. (1989). Understanding student college choice. In J. C. Smart (Ed.), *Higher education: Handbook of theory and research* (Vol. 5, pp. 231–288). New York: Agathon.

Hossler, D., and Gallagher, K. S. (1987). Studying student college choice: A three-phase model and the implications for policymakers. *College and University, 62*(3), 207–221.

Hossler, D., Schmit, J., and Vesper, N. (1999). *Going to college: How social, economic, and educational factors influence the decisions students make.* Baltimore: Johns Hopkins University Press.

Hossler, D., and Stage, F. K. (1992). Family and high school experience influences on the postsecondary educational plans of ninth-grade students. *American Educational Research Journal, 29*(2), 425–451.

Hossler, D., and Vesper, N. (1993). An exploratory study of the factors associated with parental saving for postsecondary education. *Journal of Higher Education, 64*(2), 140–165.

Hurtado, S., Inkelas, K. K., Briggs, C., and Rhee, B. S. (1997). Differences in college access and choice among racial/ethnic groups: Identifying continuing barriers. *Research in Higher Education, 38*(1), 43–75.

Ikenberry, S.O., and Hartle, T. W. (1998). *Too little knowledge is a dangerous thing: What the public thinks and knows about paying for college.* Washington, DC: American Council on Education.

Immerwahr, J. (2003). *With diploma in hand: Hispanic high school seniors talk about their future.* NCPPHE-R-03-2. San Jose, CA: National Center for Public Policy and Higher Education.

Jackson, G. A. (1986). MISSA, the fall of Saigon, and college choice: 1972–1980. Paper presented at the annual meeting of the Association for the Study of Higher Education, San Antonio, TX.

Johnson, R., and Stewart, N. (1991). Counselor impact on college choice. *School Counselor, 39*(2), 84–91.

Kao, G., and Thompson, J. S. (2003). Racial and ethnic stratification in education achievement and attainment. *Annual Review of Sociology, 29,* 417–442.

Kao, G., and Tienda, M. (1998). Educational aspirations of minority youth. *American Journal of Education, 106,* 349–384.

Karen, D. (2002). Changes in access to higher education in the United States: 1980–1992. *Sociology of Education, 75*(3), 191–210.

Kaufman, J., and Gabler, J. (2004). Cultural capital and the extracurricular activities of girls and boys in the college attainment process. *Poetics, 32,* 145–168.

Keane, M. P. (2002). Financial aid, borrowing constraints, and college attendance: Evidence from structural estimates. *American Economic Association (Papers and Proceedings), 92*(2), 293–297.

Kern, C. W. (2000). College choice influences: Urban high school students respond. *Community College Journal of Research and Practice, 24,* 487–494.

Kim, D. (2004). The effect of financial aid on students' college choice: Differences by racial groups. *Research in Higher Education, 45*(1), 43–70.

Kirst, M. W., and Bracco, K. R. (2004). Bridging the great divide: How the K–12 and postsecondary split hurts students, and what can be done about it. In M. W. Kirst and A. Venezia (Eds.), *From high school to college: Improving opportunities for success in postsecondary education* (pp. 1–30). San Francisco: Jossey-Bass.

Knight, M. G., Norton, N.E.L., Bentley, C. C., and Dixon, I. R. (2004). The power of black and Latina/o counterstories: Urban families and college-going processes. *Anthropology & Education Quarterly, 35*(1), 99–120.

Kodde, D. A., and Ritzen, J.M.M. (1988). Direct and indirect effects of parental education level on the demand for higher education. *Journal of Human Resources, 23*(3), 356–371.

Kotler, P., and Fox, K.F.A. (1985). *Strategic marketing for educational institutions.* Englewood Cliffs, NJ: Prentice Hall.

Kurlaender, M. (2006). Choosing community college: Factors affecting Latino college choice. *New Directions for Community Colleges, 133*, 7–16.

Lareau, A. (1987). Social class differences in family-school relationships: The importance of cultural capital. *Sociology of Education, 60*(2), 73–85.

Lareau, A. (2000). *Home advantage: Social class and parental intervention in elementary education* (2nd ed.). Lanham, MD: Rowman & Littlefield.

Lee, V. E., and Ekstrom, R. B. (1987). Student access to guidance counseling in high school. *American Educational Research Journal, 24*(2), 287–310.

Leslie, L. L., and Brinkman, P. T. (1987). Student price response in higher education: The student demand studies. *Journal of Higher Education, 58*(2), 181–204.

Lillard, D., and Gerner, J. (1999). Getting to the Ivy League: How family composition affects college choice. *Journal of Higher Education, 70*(6), 706–730.

Lillis, M. P. (2008). High-tuition, high-loan financing: Economic segregation in postsecondary education. *Journal of Education Finance, 34*(1), 15–30.

Litten, L. H. (1982). Different strokes in the applicant pool: Some refinements in a model of student college choice. *Journal of Higher Education, 53*(4), 383–402.

Litten, L. H., and Hall, A. E. (1989). In the eyes of our beholders: Some evidence on how high-school students and their parents view quality in colleges. *Journal of Higher Education, 60*(3), 302–324.

Lopez-Turley, R. N., Santos, M., and Ceja, C. (2007). Social origin and college opportunity expectations across cohorts. *Social Science Research, 36*, 1200–1218.

Lucas, S. R., and Good, A. D. (2001). Race, class, and tournament track mobility. *Sociology of Education, 74*(2), 139–156.

Manski, C. F., and Wise, D. A. (1983). *College choice in America.* Boston: Harvard University Press.

Mare, R. D. (1997). *Differential fertility, intergenerational mobility, and racial inequality.* National Science Foundation Report CDE-WP-97-03. Washington, DC: Office of the Assistant Secretary for Planning and Evaluation.

Martin, N. K., and Dixon, P. N. (1991). Factors influencing students' college choice. *Journal of College Student Development, 32*, 253–257.

McDonough, P. M. (1994). Buying and selling higher education: The social construction of the college applicant. *Journal of Higher Education, 65*(4), 427–446.

McDonough, P. M. (1997). *Choosing colleges: How social class and schools structure opportunity.* Albany, NY: SUNY Press.

McDonough, P. M. (1998). Structuring college opportunities: A cross-case analysis of organizational cultures, climates, and habiti. In C. A. Torres and T. R. Mitchell (Eds.), *Sociology of education: Emerging perspectives* (pp. 181–224). Albany, NY: SUNY Press.

McDonough, P. M., Antonio, A. L., and Horvat, E. M. (1996, November). College choice as capital conversation and investment: A new model. Paper presented at the annual meeting of the Association for the Study of Higher Education, Memphis, TN.

McDonough, P. M., Antonio, A. L., and Trent, J. W. (1997). Black students, black colleges: An African American college choice model. *Journal for a Just and Caring Education, 3*(1), 9–36.

McDonough, P. M., Antonio, A. L., Walpole, M., and Perez, L. X. (1998). College rankings: Democratized knowledge for whom? *Research in Higher Education, 39*(5), 513–537.

McDonough, P. M., Korn, J., and Yamasaki, E. (1997). Access, equity, and the privatization of college counseling. *Review of Higher Education, 20*(3), 297–317.

McDonough, P. M., Ventresca, M. J., and Outcalt, C. (2000). Field of dreams: Organization field approaches to understanding the transformation of college access, 1965–1995. In J. C. Smart and W. G. Tierney (Eds.), *Higher education: Handbook of theory and research* (Vol. 15, pp. 371–405). New York: Agathon.

McGrath, D. J., Swisher, R. R., Elder, G.H., Jr., and Conger, R.D. (2001). Breaking new ground: Diverse routes to college in rural America. *Rural Sociology, 66*(2), 244–267.

McPherson, M. S., and Shapiro, M. O. (1991). *The student aid game: Meeting need and rewarding talent in American higher education.* Princeton, NJ: Princeton University Press.

Mickelson, R. A. (1990). The attitude-achievement paradox among black adolescents. *Sociology of Education, 63*(1), 44–61.

Morgan, S. L. (1996). Trends in black-white differences in educational expectations: 1980–92. *Sociology of Education, 69*(1), 208–319.

Morgan, S. L. (2002). Modeling preparatory commitment and nonrepeatable decisions: Information-processing, preference formation, and educational attainment. *Rationality and Society, 14*(4), 387–429.

Muhammad, C. G. (2008). African American students and college choice: A consideration of the role of school counselors. *NASSP Bulletin, 92*(2), 81–94.

Mullen, A. L. (2009). Elite destinations: Pathways to attending an Ivy League university. *British Journal of Sociology of Education, 31*(1), 15–27.

Nora, A. (2002). A theoretical and practical view of student adjustment and academic achievement. In W. G. Tierney and L. S. Hagedorn (Eds.), *Increasing access to college: Extending possibilities for all students* (pp. 65–77). Albany, NY: SUNY Press.

Nora, A. (2004). The role of habitus and cultural capital in choosing a college, transitioning from high school to higher education, and persisting in college among minority and non-minority students. *Journal of Hispanic Higher Education, 3*(2), 180–208.

Paulsen, M. B. (1990). *College choice: Understanding student enrollment behavior.* ASHE-ERIC Higher Education Report (No. 6). Washington, DC: School of Education and Human Development, The George Washington University.

Paulsen, M. B. and St. John, E. P. (2002). Social class and college costs: Examining the financial nexus between college choice and persistence. *Journal of Higher Education, 73*(2), 189–236.

Perez, P. A., and McDonough, P. M. (2008). Understanding Latina and Latino college choice: A social capital and chain migration analysis. *Journal of Hispanic Higher Education, 7*(3), 249–265.

Perna, L. W. (2000). Differences in the decisions to attend college among African Americans, Hispanics, and whites. *Journal of Higher Education, 71*(2), 117–141.

Perna, L. W. (2005a). The benefits of higher education: Sex, racial/ethnic, and socioeconomic group differences. *Review of Higher Education, 29*(1), 23–52.

Perna, L. W. (2005b). The key to college access: Rigorous academic preparation. In W. G. Tierney, Z. B. Corwin, and J. E. Colyar (Eds.), *Preparing for college: Nine elements of effective outreach* (pp. 113–134). Albany, NY: SUNY Press.

Perna, L. W. (2006). Studying college access and choice: A proposed conceptual model. In J. C. Smart (Ed.), *Higher education: Handbook of theory and research* (Vol. 21, pp. 99–157). Amsterdam, The Netherlands: Springer.

Perna, L. W., and others. (2008). The role of college counseling in shaping college opportunity: Variations across high schools. *Review of Higher Education, 31*(2), 131–159.

Perna, L. W., Steele, P., Woda, S., and Hibbert, T. (2005). State public policies and the racial/ethnic stratification of college access and choice in the state of Maryland. *Review of Higher Education, 28*(2), 245–272.

Perna, L. W., and Titus, M. A. (2004). Understanding differences in the choice of college attended: The role of state public policies. *Review of Higher Education, 27*(4), 501–525.

Perna, L. W., and Titus, M. A. (2005). The relationship between parental involvement as social capital and college enrollment: An examination of racial/ethnic group differences. *Journal of Higher Education, 76*(5), 485–518.

Person, A. E., and Rosenbaum, J. E. (2006). Chain enrollment and college enclaves: Benefits and drawbacks of Latino college students' enrollment decisions. In C. L. Horn, S. Flores, and G. Orfield (Eds.), *New Directions for Community Colleges* (Vol. 131, pp. 51–60). San Francisco: Jossey-Bass.

Pitre, P. E. (2006a). College choice: A study of African American and white student aspirations and perceptions related to college attendance. *College Student Journal, 40*(3), 562–574.

Pitre, P. E. (2006b). Understanding predisposition in college choice: Toward an integrated model of college choice and theory of reasoned action. *College and University Journal, 81*(2), 35–42.

Plank, S. B., and Jordan, W. J. (2001). Effects of information, guidance, and actions on postsecondary destinations: A study of talent loss. *American Educational Research Journal, 38*(4), 947–979.

Post, D. (1990). College-going decisions by Chicanos: The politics of misinformation. *Educational Evaluation and Policy Analysis, 12*(2), 174–187.

Postsecondary Education Opportunity. (2008, June). *Family income and higher education opportunity.* No. 192, Oskaloosa, IA: Postsecondary Education Opportunity.

Radford, A. W., Tasoff, S., and Weko, T. (2009). Issue tables. NCES 2009-186. Washington, DC: U.S. Department of Education.

Ramirez, A. Y. (2001). "Parent involvement is like apple pie": A look at parental involvement in two states. *High School Journal, 85*(1), 1–9.

Reay, D. (2004)."It's all becoming habitus": Beyond the habitual use of habitus in educational research. *British Journal of Sociology of Education, 25*(4), 431–444.

Reay, D., Davies, J., David, M., and Ball, S. J. (2001). Choices of degree or degrees of choice? Class, "race," and the higher education choice process. *Sociology, 35*(4), 855–874.

Reynolds, J. R., and Pemberton, J. (2001). Rising college expectations among youth in the United States: A comparison of 1979 and 1997 NLSY. *Journal of Human Resources, 36*(4), 703–726.

Rosenbaum, J. E., Miller, S. R., and Krei, M. S. (1996). Gatekeeping in an era of more open gates: High school counselors' view of their influence on students' college plans. *American Journal of Education, 104*(4), 257–279.

Rowan-Kenyon, H. T., Bell, A. D., and Perna, L. W. (2008). Contextual influences on parental involvement in college going: Variations by social class. *Journal of Higher Education, 79*(5), 564–586.

St. John, E. P. (1990). Price response in enrollment decisions: An analysis of the high school and beyond sophomore cohort. *Research in Higher Education, 31*(2), 161–176.

St. John, E. P. (1994). Assessing tuition and student aid strategies: Using price-response measures to simulate pricing alternatives. *Research in Higher Education 35*(3), 301–335.

St. John, E. P., and Asker, E. H. (2001). The role of finances in student choice: A review of theory and research. In M. B. Paulsen and J. C. Smart (Eds.), *The finance of higher education: Theory, research, policy, and practice* (pp. 419–438). New York: Agathon.

St. John, E. P., and Noell, J. (1989). The effects of student financial aid on access to higher education: An analysis of progress with special consideration of minority enrollment. *Research in Higher Education, 30*(6), 563–581.

Sanders, N. F. (1990). Understanding seniors' college choices. *Journal of College Admissions, 126*, 3–8.

Schmit, J. (November, 1991). An empirical look at the search stage of the student college choice process. Paper presented at the annual meeting of the Association for the Study of Higher Education, Boston, MA.

Sissel, P. A., Hansman, C. A., and Kasworm, C. E. (2001). The politics of neglect: Adult learners in higher education. *New Directions for Adult and Continuing Education, 91*, 17–27.

Smith, H. (2007). Playing a different game: The contextualized decision-making processes of minority ethnic students in choosing a higher education institution. *Race, Ethnicity, and Education, 10*(4), 415–437.

Smith, K. (1990). A comparison of the college decisions of two-year and four-year college students. *College and University, 65*(2), 109–125.

Solorzano, D.G. (1992). An exploratory analysis of the effects of race, class, and gender on student and parent mobility aspirations. *Journal of Negro Education, 61*(1), 30–44.

Solorzano, D. G., and Ornelas, A. (2004). A critical race analysis of Latina/o and African American advanced placement enrollment in public high schools. *High School Journal, 87*(3), 15–26.

Stanton-Salazar, R. D., and Dornbusch, S. M. (1995). Social capital and the reproduction of inequality: Information networks among Mexican-origin high school students. *Sociology of Education, 68*(2), 116–135.

Stanton-Salazar, R. D., and Spina, S. U. (2000). The network orientations of highly resilient urban minority youth: A network-analytic account of minority socialization and its educational implications. *Urban Review, 32*(3), 227–261.

Stewart, M. A, and Post, P. (1990). Minority students' perceptions of variables affecting their selection of a large university. *Journal of Multicultural Counseling and Development, 18*(4), 154–162.

Swail, W. S. (2000). Preparing America's disadvantaged for college: Programs that increase college opportunity. *New Directions for Institutional Research, 107,* 85–101.

Swail, W. S., and Perna, L. W. (2002). Precollege outreach programs: A national perspective. In W. G. Tierney and L. S. Hagedorn (Eds.), *Increasing access to college: Extending possibilities for all students.* Albany, NY: SUNY Press.

Swartz, D. (1997). *Culture and power: The sociology of Pierre Bourdieu.* Chicago: University of Chicago Press.

Teranishi, R. T. (2002). Asian Pacific Americans and critical race theory: An examination of school racial climate. *Equity and Excellence in Education, 35*(2), 144–154.

Teranishi, R. T., Allen, W. R., and Solorzano, D. G. (2004). Opportunity at the crossroads: Racial inequality, school segregation, and higher education in California. *Teachers College Record, 106* (11), 2224–2245.

Teranishi, R. T., and others. (2004). The college-choice process for Asian Pacific Americans: Ethnicity and socioeconomic class in context. *Review of Higher Education, 27*(4), 427–551.

Terenzini, P. T., Cabrera, A. F., and Bernal, E. M. (2001). *Swimming against the tide: The poor in American higher education.* College Board Research Report No. 1. New York: College Entrance Examination Board.

Tierney, M. I. (1982). The impact of institutional net price on student demand for public and private higher education. *Economics of Education Review, 2*(4), 363–383.

Tierney, W. G. (2002). Parents and families in precollege preparation: The lack of connection between research and practice. *Educational Policy, 16*(4), 588–606.

Tierney, W. G., and Jun, A. (2001). A university helps prepare low-income youths for college: Tracking school success. *Journal of Higher Education, 72*(2), 205–225.

Tierney, W. G., and Venegas, K. M. (2009). Finding money on the table: Information, financial aid, and access to college. *Journal of Higher Education, 80*(4), 363–388.

U.S. Department of Education. (2005). *Postsecondary participation rates by sex and race/ethnicity: 1974–2003.* Report No, 2005-028. Washington, DC: National Center for Education Statistics.

Valencia, R. R. (Ed.). (1997). *The evolution of deficit thinking: Educational thought and practice.* Washington, DC: Falmer Press.

Van der Klaaw, W. (2002). Estimating the effect of financial aid offers on college enrollment: A regression-discontinuity approach. *International Economic Review, 43*(4), 1249–1287.

Villalpando, O., and Solorzano, D. G. (2005). The role of culture in college preparation programs: A review of the research literature. In W. G. Tierney, Z. B. Corwin, and J. E. Colyar (Eds.), *Preparing for college: Nine elements of effective outreach* (pp. 13–28). Albany, NY: SUNY Press.

Walpole, M. (2003). Socioeconomic status and college: How SES affects college experiences and outcomes. *Review of Higher Education, 27*(1), 45–73.

Walpole, M. (2007). *Economically and educationally challenged students in higher education: Access and outcomes.* ASHE Higher Education Report. Vol. 33, No. 3. San Francisco: Jossey-Bass.

Wolniak, G. C., and Engberg, M. E. (2007). The effects of high school feeder networks on college enrollment. *Review of Higher Education, 31*(1), 27–53.

Name Index

K

Kane, T. J., 15, 23, 51
Kao, G., 13, 29, 66, 67, 76, 111, 112
Karen, D., 52, 109, 110
Kasworm, C. E., 7
Kaufman, J., 36, 54
Keane, M. P., 51
Keller, J. E., 87, 90
Kern, C. W., 35, 48
Kim, D., 28, 36, 78
Kinser, K., 7
Kirst, M. W., 87
Knight, M. G., 75, 76, 103
Kodde, D. A., 4
Korn, J., 23, 104, 110
Kostal, T., 108
Kotler, P., 5, 17
Koyama, J. P., 23, 73
Krei, M. S., 23
Kurlaender, M., 78, 79

L

LaNasa, S. M., 13, 21, 22, 23, 24, 25, 26,
   27, 29, 35, 36–37, 48, 51, 52, 53, 104,
   105, 106, 107
Lara, C. M., 27
Lareau, A., 55
Lee, V. E., 3
Leslie, L. L., 4, 21
Lillard, D., 21, 31
Lillis, M. P., 19, 23, 28, 108
Litten, L. H., 3, 5, 17, 21
Lopez-Turley, R. N., 29, 51, 52, 76
Lucas, S. R., 30, 70, 71, 81

M

Manski, C. F., 3, 4
Mare, R. D., 48
Mark, M. C., 25, 26, 32
Martin, N. K., 24, 29, 32
McCall, B. P., 21, 25, 28, 33
McDonough, P. M., 13, 14, 23, 26, 29, 34,
   42, 54, 55, 56, 57, 58, 59, 60, 74, 79,
   103, 104, 108, 109, 110
McGrath, D. J., 52

McLoyd, V. C., 69, 105
McPherson, M. S., 23, 28, 78
Mickelson, R. A., 14, 29, 79, 96
Miller, S. R., 23
Moore, D. E., 87, 90
Morgan, S. L., 23, 29, 38, 39
Morphew, C. C., 21, 26
Muhammad, C. G., 23, 71, 105
Mullen, A. L., 30, 58, 104

N

Noell, J., 4
Nora, A., 21, 29, 33, 49, 58, 94
Norton, N.E.L., 75, 76, 103

O

Ornelas, A., 9, 13, 18, 30, 72, 105
Otto, L. B., 3
Outcalt, C., 34, 57, 109

P

Pauls, K., 29
Paulsen, M. B., 1, 2, 3, 4, 8, 9, 11–12, 19,
   25, 28, 36, 51, 78, 80, 99, 100, 101,
   102, 107, 112, 113, 115
Pemberton, J., 29, 48
Perez, L. X., 14, 23, 34
Perez, P. A., 74
Perna, L. W., 13–14, 18, 19, 21, 22, 23,
   24, 27, 28, 29, 30, 34, 37, 38, 46, 49,
   51, 53, 55, 56, 57, 62, 65, 70, 71, 77,
   79, 81, 86, 92, 93, 96, 104, 107, 108,
   109, 110, 111, 112
Person, A. E., 26, 74
Pitre, P. E., 14, 18, 29, 39, 40, 66, 70,
   71, 107
Plank, S. B., 26, 80
Post, D., 28
Post, P., 21, 29, 79

R

Radford, A. W, 12, 13
Ramirez, A. Y., 23
Reay, D., 28, 29, 36, 41, 51
Reynolds, J. R., 29, 48

Rhee, B. S., 6, 16, 30, 32, 47, 80, 81, 107
Ritblatt, W. N., 23, 30
Ritzen, J.M.M., 4
Rosenbaum, J. E., 23, 26, 74
Rowan-Kenyon, H. T., 30, 81

S

Sanders, N. F., 21, 29
Santos, M., 29, 51, 52, 76
Schmit, J., 22, 24, 25, 26, 27, 28, 29, 32, 34, 49
Shapiro, M. O., 23, 28, 78
Singell, L. D., Jr., 28, 33
Sissel, P. A., 7
Slavin, R. E., 91
Smith, H., 21, 29, 60, 79, 104, 105
Smith, K., 29
Solorzano, D. G., 9, 13, 18, 22, 29, 30, 45, 65, 66, 70, 72, 82, 85, 95, 104, 105, 109, 110, 112
Spina, S. U., 73, 74, 81
St. John, E. P., 4, 25, 28, 36, 51, 78, 80
Stage, F. K., 21, 22, 23, 31, 48, 49, 67, 69, 105, 111, 112
Stanton-Salazar, R. D., 26, 73, 74, 81
Steele, P., 14, 19, 51, 107
Stewart, M. A., 21, 29, 79
Stewart, N., 26, 29, 79
Stoner, C., 18, 45, 53, 56, 58, 69, 71, 80, 105, 106
Swail, W. S., 86
Swartz, D., 42
Swisher, R. R., 52

T

Tasoff, S., 12, 13

Teranishi, R. T., 6, 15, 16, 21, 72
Terenzini, P. T., 13, 26
Thompson, J. S., 13, 76, 111
Thompson, S., 48
Tienda, M., 29, 66, 67, 112
Tierney, M. I., 4
Tierney, W. G., 4, 9, 18, 23, 27, 38, 40, 46, 54, 75, 76, 85, 87, 88, 89, 91, 92, 93, 94, 95, 96, 97, 103, 104
Titus, M. A., 19, 22, 23, 28, 34, 55, 104, 107, 108, 109, 112
Trent, J. W., 60, 79, 108

V

Valdez, S., 27
Valencia, R. R., 44
Van der Klaaw, W., 33
Venegas, K. M., 38, 40, 46
Ventresca, M. J., 34, 57, 109
Vesper, N., 22, 24, 25, 26, 27, 28, 29, 32, 34, 49
Villalpando, O., 9, 22, 45, 82, 85, 95, 104

W

Wacquant, L.J.D., 41, 43
Walpole, M., 26, 29, 34
Weko, T., 12, 13
Wise, D. A., 3, 4
Woda, S., 14, 19, 51, 107
Wolniak, G. C., 30

Y

Yamasaki, E., 23, 104, 110

Subject Index

A

Abstract attitudes, in students of color, 65

Academic achievement: and enrollment decisions, 23, 30, 71; impact of peers on Latino and white students, 72–74

Academic preparation, college preparation and access programs, 92–93

Advancement via Individual Determination (AVID), 26, 86, 89–90; academic preparation, 93; and cultural scaffolding, 95; and family involvement in students' educational planning, 96; information access, 94

African American students: academic preparation, 81; aspirations, 66; capital, access to, 56; college attendance decisions, 53; college choice experiences, 16–17; college-going behaviors, 40; and college's geographical location, 74–75; and cultural relevancy, 71; decision to attend college, 70; decline in enrollment (1976 to 1986), 79; distinctive experiences of, 111; educational expectations, impact of, 53; enrollment rates, 55; family background characteristics, 70; family socioeconomic status, 69; feelings of mistrust toward educational systems, 71; fit, importance of, 79–80; future policy toward, 108; and high school personnel, 80; marginalization and lack of participation in higher education, 17; and

Neighborhood Academic Initiative (NAI), 91; parents' expectations, 67–68; participation in postsecondary education, 15; postsecondary education choice processes, 16–17; presence in community colleges, 79; price paid for social mobility, 61; school personnel and stereotypical assumptions, 59; and school personnel stereotypes, 59–60; segregated schools, 112; sensitivity to cost of education, 77, 79; social and cultural capital, 56, 60; structured counseling, 27; white students' college choice process compared to, 81

ASHE-ERIC Higher Education Report (Paulsen), 1, 3

Asian Pacific American students, college choices of (study), 6

Asian students, 6, 12, 15; geographic location of school, 79; high-status habitus, 59; information access, 59, 80; over-achievement of, 67; parents' education level, 76; presence in community colleges, 79

Aspirations: college preparation and access programs, 94–95; and high school experiences, 70–71; impact of peers on Latino and white students, 72–74; of Mexican American students compared to European American students, 67; in students of color, 65–67

AVID, *See* Advancement via Individual Determination (AVID)

outcomes, 22; critiques of, 34–36; predisposition stage, 22–24; in recent research, 30–33; search phase, 24–27

I

I Have a Dream (IHAD), 86, 89–90; academic preparedness, 93; and college-going aspirations and self-efficacy, 94–95; and family involvement in students' educational planning, 96; financial aid, 96; information access, 94
Information access: and college choice, 57–58; college preparation and access programs, 93–94
Intended audience, monograph, 6–7

K

K–12 schooling experiences, inequities in, and student ability, 19

L

Language, and students of color, 45
Latina and Latino students, 79, *See also* Hispanic students; academic preparation, 80–81; and college preparation programs, 103–104; and college's geographical location, 74; downward track mobility, 103; educational expectations, and access to agents of social capital, 58, 80; family and peer networks, 74–75; high school personnel, access to, 18; and High School Puente, 86, 91; institutional agents and barriers for college attendance, 56; limited postsecondary opportunities, 105; parental support of educational aspirations, 53; peer networks, 74–75; peer networks for, 74; presence in community colleges, 78–79; social capital, access to, 58, 69, 71
Loan-based financial aid, trend toward, 79
Lower socioeconomic students: access to capital, relationship between academic preparation and, 56; college choice for, 47–62; cost sensitivity, 51; differences in the schooling experiences of, 55;

financial aid/costs, 77–80; issues of access for, 47–50; and loans to finance a college education, 19–20

M

Mathematics, Engineering, Science Achievement (MESA), 86, 89–91; academic preparedness, 93; and family involvement in students' educational planning, 96; information access, 94
McGrath, Patricia, 91
Mexican American students: with higher socioeconomic backgrounds, 72–73; parental engagement with children's education, 68–69
Monograph: intended audience, 6–7; limitations of, 7–8; organization of, 8–9

N

National Science Foundation, 86
Native American students, presence in community colleges, 79
Neighborhood Academic Initiative (NAI), 86, 89, 91; academic preparedness, 93; and cultural scaffolding, 95; and family involvement in students' educational planning, 96; financial aid and financial planning, 91; information access, 94
Normative commitment, 39

O

Overachievement of Asian students, 67

P

Parents: education of, and students' ability to gain qualifications necessary for enrollment in higher education, 51–52; encouragement of, and educational expectations, 53–54; engagement with children's education, 68–69; expectations, and predisposition, 67–68; networks, and college enrollment, 52–53
Parental influence: institutional quality expectations, 24–25; knowledge and understanding of the costs/availability of

financial aid, 25; parental encouragement, 24–25, 29; price and proximity as parental signals, 24

Paulsen's recommendations for practice, 100–101; enrollment patterns, 100; environmental factors, effect on enrollment behaviors, 100; stratification of higher education, 101

Paulsen's recommendations for research and policy, 101–102; nontraditional students, 101; search process, 101; state and federal involvement in research and policy involvement, 102

Peer networks, for Latina and Latino students, 74

Perna's conceptual model, 37

Pitre college choice model, 40

Policy focus, increases in, 19

Practice, policy, and research: from current research, 102–113; equity in college preparedness, 114–115; increased focus on, 115; Paulsen's recommendations for practice, 100–101; Paulsen's recommendations for research and policy, 101–102; recommendations for (from 1989), 99–118; stages in college choice process, 114; students' experiences of the college choice process, 115–116; trend toward addressing issues of access and equity in the choice process, 114

Predisposition: and high school experiences of, 70–72; and parents' expectations, 67–68; and socioeconomic status, 69–70; students of color, 64–75

Preparation for college, 17–19

Price sensitivity, 4

Process models: characteristics of, 21; defined, 21; three-stage model of Hossler and Gallagher, 21, 22–30

Psychosocial factors, in institutional choices, 33

Purposive commitment, 39

R

Race, and the college choice process, 110–111

Recommendations: policy, 106–110; practice, 102–106

Relevancy, cultural, and African American students, 71

Research, college choice, current trends in, 11–20; future, recommendations for, 110–113; recommendations for research and policy, 102–113

Research horizons, broadening, 112–113

Review of college choice body of research, 11; limitations of, 7–8

S

Social capital, 42, 52

Social class status, and the college choice process, 62, 110–111

Social reproduction theory, 41, 42–44, 59; cultural capital, 42–43; economic capital, 42; field, 43; habitus, 41–42; social capital, 42

Stanford Bridge Project, 87

Student price sensitivity, 4

Student Support services, 86, 89

Students of color: abstract attitudes, and predisposition, 65; and access/equity, 60; aspirations, 65–67; barriers to predisposition, 75; college choice processes for, 63–84; college choices of (study), 6; concrete attitudes, and predisposition, 65; deficit explanation for underrepresentation in higher education, 44; educational aspirations and expectations, role in predisposition, 64–65; family-related factors in college enrollment, 75–76; financial aid/costs, 77–80; geographic location, 79–80; increasing access to higher education for, 44–45; and language, 45; and loans to finance a college education, 19–20; parent income and education, 76–77; parental engagement with children's education, 68–69; parental expectations, 67–68; parental involvement in enrollment, 77; predisposition, 64–75; price paid for social mobility, 61; research related to college choice, 64–82; socioeconomic status, and predisposition, 69–70

T

Talent Search, 86, 89; and college-going aspirations and self-efficacy, 94–95

Tierney and Venegas's cultural framework model, 38

Trends: away from comprehensive models of college choice, 11–12; in college choice research, 11–20; toward addressing issues of access and equity in the choice process, 114; toward loan-based financial aid, 79;

TRIO programs, 86, 87, 89–90; and financial planning, 96

U

Upper-income students, parents' networks and college enrollment, 52–53

Upward Bound, 26, 86, 89; academic preparedness, 93; information access, 94

U.S. Department of Education, 15

V

Viewing the college choice process, alternative lenses for, 41–45

W

Wealth, cultural, 44–45; argument for bilingual capability, 45

White students: college choice process compared to African American students, 81; impact of peers on, 72–74

About the Author

Amy Aldous Bergerson is an assistant professor in the Department of Educational Leadership and Policy at the University of Utah. She holds a B.A. in sociology from Amherst College, an M.A. in educational administration and policy analysis from Stanford University, and a Ph.D. in educational leadership and policy with an emphasis on higher education from the University of Utah. Her research focuses on college choice, college student retention, and social justice in higher education. Several years of administrative experience in higher education shape Bergerson's research and teaching interests and her work with graduate students. Bergerson is active in several national organizations and serves as a reviewer for a number of academic journals.

About the ASHE Higher Education Report Series

Since 1983, the ASHE (formerly ASHE-ERIC) Higher Education Report Series has been providing researchers, scholars, and practitioners with timely and substantive information on the critical issues facing higher education. Each monograph presents a definitive analysis of a higher education problem or issue, based on a thorough synthesis of significant literature and institutional experiences. Topics range from planning to diversity and multiculturalism, to performance indicators, to curricular innovations. The mission of the Series is to link the best of higher education research and practice to inform decision making and policy. The reports connect conventional wisdom with research and are designed to help busy individuals keep up with the higher education literature. Authors are scholars and practitioners in the academic community. Each report includes an executive summary, review of the pertinent literature, descriptions of effective educational practices, and a summary of key issues to keep in mind to improve educational policies and practice.

The Series is one of the most peer reviewed in higher education. A National Advisory Board made up of ASHE members reviews proposals. A National Review Board of ASHE scholars and practitioners reviews completed manuscripts. Six monographs are published each year and they are approximately 120 pages in length. The reports are widely disseminated through Jossey-Bass and John Wiley & Sons, and they are available online to subscribing institutions through Wiley InterScience (http://www.interscience.wiley.com).

Call for Proposals

The ASHE Higher Education Report Series is actively looking for proposals. We encourage you to contact one of the editors, Dr. Kelly Ward (kaward@wsu.edu) or Dr. Lisa Wolf-Wendel (lwolf@ku.edu), with your ideas.

Recent Titles

ASHE HIGHER EDUCATION REPORT

ORDER FORM SUBSCRIPTION AND SINGLE ISSUES

DISCOUNTED BACK ISSUES:

Use this form to receive 20% off all back issues of *ASHE Higher Education Report*.
All single issues priced at **$23.20** (normally $29.00)

TITLE	ISSUE NO.	ISBN

Call 888-378-2537 or see mailing instructions below. When calling, mention the promotional code JBXND to receive your discount. For a complete list of issues, please visit www.josseybass.com/go/aehe

SUBSCRIPTIONS: (1 YEAR, 6 ISSUES)

☐ New Order   ☐ Renewal

U.S.	☐ Individual: $174	☐ Institutional: $244
CANADA/MEXICO	☐ Individual: $174	☐ Institutional: $304
ALL OTHERS	☐ Individual: $210	☐ Institutional: $355

Call 888-378-2537 or see mailing and pricing instructions below.
Online subscriptions are available at www.interscience.wiley.com

ORDER TOTALS:

Issue / Subscription Amount: $ _____

Shipping Amount: $ _____
(for single issues only – subscription prices include shipping)

Total Amount: $ _____

SHIPPING CHARGES:		
SURFACE	DOMESTIC	CANADIAN
First Item	$5.00	$6.00
Each Add'l Item	$3.00	$1.50

(No sales tax for U.S. subscriptions. Canadian residents, add GST for subscription orders. Individual rate subscriptions must be paid by personal check or credit card. Individual rate subscriptions may not be resold as library copies.)

BILLING & SHIPPING INFORMATION:

☐ **PAYMENT ENCLOSED:** *(U.S. check or money order only. All payments must be in U.S. dollars.)*

☐ **CREDIT CARD:** ☐ VISA ☐ MC ☐ AMEX

Card number _____ Exp. Date_____

Card Holder Name_____ Card Issue # *(required)* _____

Signature _____ Day Phone_____

☐ **BILL ME:** *(U.S. institutional orders only. Purchase order required.)*

Purchase order # _____
Federal Tax ID 13559302 • GST 89102-8052

Name_____

Address_____

Phone_____ E-mail_____

Copy or detach page and send to: **John Wiley & Sons, PTSC, 5th Floor**
989 Market Street, San Francisco, CA 94103-1741

Order Form can also be faxed to: **888-481-2665**

PROMO JBXND

ASHE-ERIC HIGHER EDUCATION REPORT
IS NOW AVAILABLE ONLINE AT WILEY INTERSCIENCE

What is Wiley InterScience?

Wiley InterScience is the dynamic online content service from John Wiley & Sons delivering the full text of over 300 leading scientific, technical, medical, and professional journals, plus major reference works, the acclaimed Current Protocols laboratory manuals, and even the full text of select Wiley print books online.

What are some special features of Wiley InterScience?

Wiley Interscience Alerts is a service that delivers table of contents via e-mail for any journal available on Wiley InterScience as soon as a new issue is published online.

Early View is Wiley's exclusive service presenting individual articles online as soon as they are ready, even before the release of the compiled print issue. These articles are complete, peer-reviewed, and citable.

CrossRef is the innovative multi-publisher reference linking system enabling readers to move seamlessly from a reference in a journal article to the cited publication, typically located on a different server and published by a different publisher.

How can I access Wiley InterScience?

Visit http://www.interscience.wiley.com.

Guest Users can browse Wiley InterScience for unrestricted access to journal Tables of Contents and Article Abstracts, or use the powerful search engine.

Registered Users are provided with a *Personal Home Page* to store and manage customized alerts, searches, and links to favorite journals and articles. Additionally, Registered Users can view free Online Sample Issues and preview selected material from major reference works.

Licensed Customers are entitled to access full-text journal articles in PDF, with select journals also offering full-text HTML.

How do I become an Authorized User?

Authorized Users are individuals authorized by a paying Customer to have access to the journals in Wiley InterScience. For example, a University that subscribes to Wiley journals is considered to be the Customer.

Faculty, staff and students authorized by the University to have access to those journals in Wiley InterScience are Authorized Users. Users should contact their Library for information on which Wiley journals they have access to in Wiley InterScience.

ASK YOUR INSTITUTION ABOUT WILEY INTERSCIENCE TODAY!

Why Wait to Make Great Discoveries

When you can make them in an instant with
Wiley InterScience® Pay-Per-View and ArticleSelect™

Now you can have instant, full-text access to an extensive collection of journal articles or book chapters available on Wiley InterScience. With Pay-Per-View and ArticleSelect™, there's no limit to what you can discover...

ArticleSelect™ is a token-based service, providing access to full-text content from non-subscribed journals to existing institutional customers (EAL and BAL)

Pay-per-view is available to any user, regardless of whether they hold a subscription with Wiley InterScience.

Benefits:

- Access online full-text content from journals and books that are outside your current library holdings
- Use it at home, on the road, from anywhere at any time
- Build an archive of articles and chapters targeted for your unique research needs
- Take advantage of our free profiled alerting service the perfect companion to help you find specific articles in your field as soon as they're published
- Get what you need instantly no waiting for document delivery
- Fast, easy, and secure online credit card processing for pay-per-view downloads
- Special, cost-savings for EAL customers: whenever a customer spends tokens on a title equaling 115% of its subscription price, the customer is auto-subscribed for the year
- Access is instant and available for 24 hours

WILEY
InterScience®
DISCOVER SOMETHING GREAT

www.interscience.wiley.com